# S~~P~~
# and Dalmatia

By the staff of Berlitz Guides

Copyright © 1977 by Berlitz Guides, a division of
Macmillan S.A., Avenue d'Ouchy 61, 1000 Lausanne 6, Switzerland.

All rights reserved. No part of this book may be reproduced or transmitted in any form or by any means, electronic or mechanical, including photocopying, recording or by any information storage and retrieval system without permission in writing from the publisher.

Berlitz Trademark Reg. U.S. Patent Office and other countries. Marca Registrada. Library of Congress Catalog Card No. 76-21367.

Printed in Switzerland by Weber S.A., Bienne.

**6th Printing**
**1987/1988 Edition**

# How to use our guide

- All the practical information, hints and tips that you will need before and during the trip start on page 95.
- For general background, see the sections Dalmatia, The Region and the People, p. 6, and A Brief History, p. 11.
- All the sights to see are listed between pages 18 and 72. Our own choice of sights most highly recommended is pinpointed by the Berlitz traveller symbol.
- Entertainment, nightlife and all other leisure activies are described between pages 73 and 84, while information on restaurants and cuisine is to be found on pages 85 to 94.
- Finally, there is an index at the back of the book, pp. 126–128.

---

*Although we make every effort to ensure the accuracy of all the information in this book, changes occur incessantly. We cannot therefore take responsibility for facts, prices, addresses and circumstances in general that are constantly subject to alteration. Our guides are updated on a regular basis as we reprint, and we are always grateful to readers who let us know of any errors, changes or serious omissions they come across.*

---

Text: Karin Radovanović
Photography: Erling Mandelmann
We would like to thank Naum R. Dimitrijević, Sara Crowgey and the Yugoslav National Tourist Office for their assistance.
Cartography: Falk-Verlag, Hamburg

# Contents

| | | |
|---|---|---|
| Dalmatia | The Region and the People | 6 |
| A Brief History | | 11 |
| Where to Go | | |
| | Split | 18 |
| | North of Split | 30 |
| | South of Split | 55 |
| | Islands off Split | 63 |
| What to Do | | |
| | Folklore, Festivals | 73 |
| | Nightlife | 75 |
| | Museums and Galleries | 76 |
| | For Children | 77 |
| | Shopping | 78 |
| Sports and Other Activities | | 81 |
| Wining and Dining | | 85 |
| How to Get There and When to Go | | 95 |
| **Blueprint for a Perfect Trip** (Practical Information) | | 98 |
| Index | | 126 |

## Maps

| | | |
|---|---|---|
| | Bird's-Eye View of Dalmatia | 6 |
| | Diocletian's Palace | 19 |
| | Split and Vicinity | 26 |
| | North of Split | 31 |
| | Šibenik | 37 |
| | Zadar | 45 |
| | South of Split | 56 |

# Dalmatia

## The Region and the People

Skirting a sun-warmed sea, the coast of Dalmatia* twists into countless coves and inlets hiding fishing villages, medieval walled towns and beaches for escapists. Behind the narrow coastal strip rises a barrier of rugged mountains, broken occasionally by spectacular canyons. Offshore, green-terraced islands and crags of naked rock are strewn across the sparkling Adriatic. Dalmatia is scenery on the grand scale—but also much more.

After you've sunbathed, sailed and snorkelled, put on your serious sightseeing shoes. Follow the footsteps of the Roman legions through the triumphal gates of the ancient city of Split. Explore the remains of the magnificent palace, built for the retirement of Emperor Diocletian. Over the years, the palace and town have grown into one another,

---

*Actually, Dalmatia runs from Starigrad-Paklenica north of Split, down to Oštri Rt at the Bay of Kotor, south of Dubrovnik. The Berlitz guide to DUBROVNIK AND SOUTHERN DALMATIA covers the southern part of the Yugoslav coast.

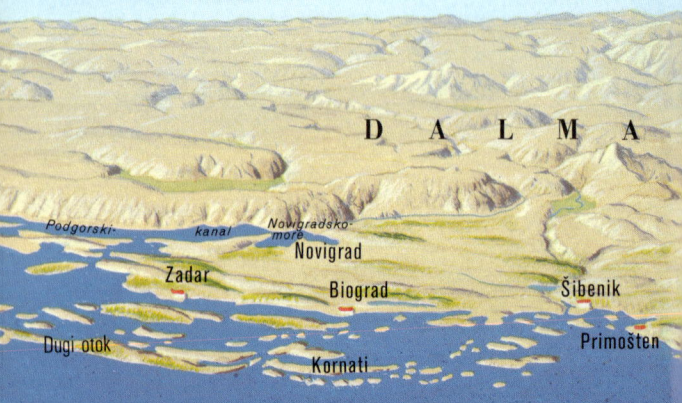

making it hard to tell where one leaves off and the other starts. Split itself is a successful mixture of art and architecture from many different centuries. Within a few blocks you may see an Egyptian sphinx, a Roman temple, Byzantine lions, Romanesque arches, a Venetian Gothic doorway, a Renaissance courtyard and a Baroque altarpiece. Find your way along the age-old streets, some so narrow you can reach out and touch the walls on either side.

Other venerable towns dot the coast to the northwest. In tiny Trogir, where time seems to have stopped centuries ago, a tangle of streets leads to a cathedral with a splendid portal. Not to be outdone, nearby Šibenik built its own lavish cathedral. Town-planning Romans laid out the first streets of Zadar, where a goodly share of medieval splendours have survived all manner of disasters.

Descending the coast from Split, the former pirates' lair of Omiš hugs the craggy slopes flanking the awesome Cetina River gorge. Farther southeast, fishing towns like Makarska, Podgora and Brela offer long, pine-fringed pebble beaches, set against the towering ridges of Biokovo.

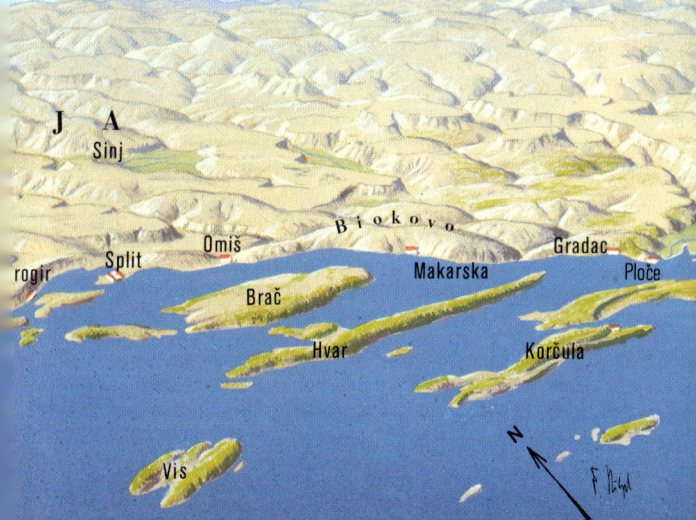

*A tempting offer of figs—freshly picked, still warm from the sun.*

Take a ferryboat to an island. The quarries of Brač furnished the stone for Diocletian's palace; more and more visitors come here to enjoy the tranquillity of its slumbering fishing villages. The beauties of Hvar have been admired for at least 3,000 years. It has a remarkably mild climate, fields of scented lavender and a town filled with Gothic and Renaissance palaces. Southernmost Korčula is another island jewel; if you time your visit well, you can see a traditional folk pageant with islanders costumed as Moors and Turks performing a dangerous sword dance.

The stretch of coastline from Zadar in the north down to Dubrovnik measures 395 kilometres on the winding Adriatic Highway *(Jadranska magistrala)*. It's all part of Croatia, one of Yugoslavia's six republics (except for a small section giving Bosnia-Herzegovina access to the sea). As you travel south, the fertile coastal belt narrows and in spots disappears with steep, jagged mountains plunging straight into the sea. The gentle, almost tideless sea washes pebble, or shingle, beaches tucked into sheltering coves. Sandy beaches are rare. Where the shore is rocky, resorts have built concrete or stone quays for sunbathing and getting easily into the water.

Dalmatia enjoys a daily average of 12 hours of sunshine in July, more than the French Riviera or Majorca. Summer temperatures fluctuate from 71° to 86°F, but even the hottest days are soothed by sea breezes. On the islands, the winter climate is so reliable that the Hvar hotels guarantee their guests free room and board for any day of snow, fog or below-freezing temperature.

Before your morning swim, watch the fishing boats returning with the night's catch of sardines. Then join the local housewives judging the grapes at the open-air market. Take a break at an outdoor café, congenial hub of day- and nightlife.

In a village, you can stay as a paying guest in somebody's house. The living is cheap, the fresh fish, salads and local wine wholesome. Or, if you prefer, splurge on total luxury in a palatial hotel with five-course meals, heated pool, sauna, bar, discotheque and gambling casino on the premises.

History has endowed this country with a diversity of nationalities, religions and languages. Political union is only a recent event. Yet, for all their differences, the farmers, fishermen, shipbuilders and artists of Yugoslavia all share an ancient tradition of hospitality. The welcome mat is out.

*Fantasy in lace, a skill handed down from a more tranquil age.*

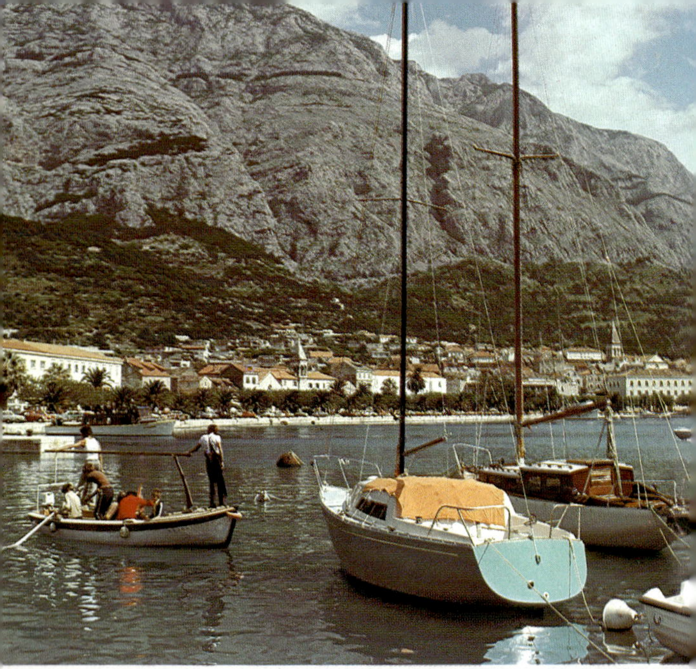

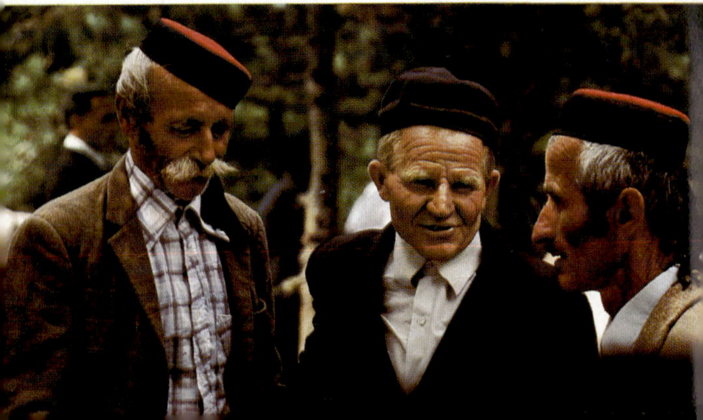

# A Brief History

The history of Yugoslavia begins thousands of years ago. Yet its peoples have formed one state only since 1918. And its name, Yugoslavia (South Slavia), is also of recent vintage.

The Adriatic shores were already inhabited in the Stone Age, perhaps 5,000 years ago. Illyrian tribes settled here during the Bronze and Iron Ages. One of them, the Dalmatae, gave its name to the region.

In the 4th century B.C., the Greeks set up trading posts on the islands of Hvar and Vis and on the mainland. By the 1st century A.D., Roman armies had conquered both the Greeks and the Illyrians. Roman rule united the territory now known as Yugoslavia—a feat that was not to be repeated for 1,500 years.

The split in the Roman empire towards the end of the 4th century A.D. affected all of the ancient world. It had a major impact on the Balkans. Present-day Serbia, Macedonia, Montenegro and most of Bosnia-Herzegovina were absorbed by the eastern empire of Constantinople; Slovenia, Croatia and Dalmatia went under the wing of Rome. The cultural and religious gulf widened during the Middle Ages when the western, Catholic regions fell, in turn, under Hungarian, Venetian and Austro-Hungarian rule, while the Orthodox areas were swallowed up by the Turkish empire. Despite the political unification of modern Yugoslavia, these ancient divisions haven't been entirely erased.

### The Dark Ages

The Dark Ages were harsh in Yugoslavia. Hordes of invaders—infamous tribes like the Goths, Huns and Vandals—swept over the land. No less barbarous were the Avars, founders of the first Mogul empire, who sacked Salona (near Split) in 614. Probably the first Slavs to set foot in Yugoslavia were warriors attached to the Avar armies.

From plunder, the invaders gradually turned to more peaceful occupations. The romanized Illyrians and the descendants of Roman settlers living along

*Never fortified, Makarska was held by the Turks for 150 years; below: hardy, outgoing people of Dalmatia.*

*An ancient sailing route extended along Dalmatia's coast and isles.*

the coast either fled to the islands or crowded for safety into fortified towns. The Slavs were left to farm the countryside.

In time, the Croats, a Slavic tribe that had settled in Dalmatia, occupied more and more of the coastland, building up a powerful naval state. Their ships challenged Venice and Byzantium for control of the eastern Adriatic. In 924, Pope John X crowned Tomislav the first king of Croatia. The kingdom lasted for almost 200 years, until its union with Hungary.

The Dalmatian towns managed to retain considerable autonomy by paying some tribute to their more powerful neighbours. But their histories are punctuated by disaster. Trogir was sacked by the Saracens and by Venice; Zadar was pillaged by the Crusaders, Biograd was completely levelled. Tartars, corsairs and Turks all had a share in the devastation of the coastal cities.

**Venetian Dominance**

In the 15th century, through a combination of sea power, diplomacy and financial dealing, Venice gained control over most of the coast. This brought a period of relative tranquillity to the cities, and art and architecture flourished. But the great days of Venice were already passing as the discovery of the New World reduced the importance of Mediterranean trade routes. Venice's hold in the Adriatic weakened, and Croatia and Dalmatia, caught between the Austrians, Hungarians, pirates and Turks, went through some very turbulent years.

In the year 1797, the Venetian republic changed hands twice: first Napoleon and then Austria held sway. Dalmatia also became part of the Hapsburg empire, remaining in Austrian hands until World War I — except for one brief and dramatic interlude in 1809 when

Napoleon took over. Following the example of the Caesars, Bonaparte renamed Dalmatia the Illyrian Province, but he showed less respect for tradition in abolishing the historical independence of the cities.

When Napoleon met his Waterloo in 1815, Austria reasserted control. Under the new regime, the prosperous Italian minority enjoyed a favoured position, which the Croats and Slovenes naturally resented. Bad feeling between Italians and Yugoslavs continued into the 20th century, involving a series of border disputes that have only recently been settled.

Croatian sentiment against the Magyars, who governed the Croats, Slovenes and Serbs of the Hapsburg empire, reached acute proportions in the latter part of the 19th century. The Hungarians attempted to force Magyarization, enraging the people and inciting the spread of Pan-Slavism. The independent state of Serbia served as an inspiration for ideas of South Slav autonomy, even independence.

*Roman aqueduct of Salona, built to carry water to Diocletian's Palace, is still working today.*

In time, the explosive situation, which grew worse as the Hapsburg regime became feeble and more desperate, affected all of European history. On June 28, 1914, Archduke Franz Ferdinand, heir to the Hapsburg empire, was assassinated in the Bosnian city of Sarajevo. The Serbian government was accused of connivance in the plot. After issuing a humiliating ultimatum which Serbia couldn't accept and urged on by a Germany which believed in dealing from strength, Austria-Hungary declared war, hoping to expand its Balkan territories. The other big powers were drawn in, and Europe marched into the horrors of World War I.

After heroically checking the Austro-Hungarian advance for over a year and, incidentally, winning the first allied victory of the war at Cer, the exhausted Serbian armies, weakened by a typhoid epidemic, short of supplies and attacked from the rear by Bulgaria, were forced to retreat across the Albanian mountains to Corfu. It was here that the concept of a united Yugoslavia, the long-cherished dream of Southern Slavs, formally took shape. In mid-summer 1917, representatives of Serbia, Croatia, Slovenia and Montenegro signed the Corfu Declaration calling for the formation of a single state under the Serbian crown in which all Yugoslav peoples would enjoy complete equality.

*This crumbling fort perched high above Omiš recalls a perilous past; right: Josip Broz Tito*

## Tumultuous Search for Unity

The years between the world wars made Yugoslavia the kind of country which inspired clichés about the Balkan tinderbox. Italian troops, implementing a secret treaty of 1915 (in which Britain, France and Russia promised these regions to Italy as part of its reward for joining the Allies in the war), occupied Istria and parts of the Dalmatian coast. In addition, failure by the Serbian-dominated government to meet the terms of the Corfu Declaration regarding national equality was a source of bitterness and discord within the young state. In 1928, the Croatian opposition leader was shot down in parliament; the following year King Alexander proclaimed a royal dictatorship, banning all political parties and nationalist organizations. It was at this time the country's name was changed to Yugoslavia. The world depression of the early 1930s was particularly hard on Yugoslavia's economy; the unemployment rate boiled to an explosive 40 per cent. In 1934, on a state visit to France, King Alexander was assassinated by a killer working for Macedonian and Croatian separatist groups.

Staggered by these disasters, and surrounded by the growing menace of Hitler and Mussolini, Yugoslavia tried to steer clear of Europe's approaching confrontations. But protestations of neutrality couldn't match the pressures. In March 1941, Prince Paul, the regent, went to Hitler's Berchtesgaden hideaway for a secret audience with the Führer. The resulting agreements pledged Yugoslavia's support for the Axis in return for the promise of Salonika (Greek Macedonia). Irate Yugoslavs sent Paul packing into exile within a matter of days. Under popular pressure, the new government renounced the Axis pact, so enraging Hitler that he declared he would wipe Yugoslavia off the map.

On April 6, 1941, without a formal declaration of war, the Luftwaffe bombed Belgrade;

Axis troops rolled across five frontiers. Ill-prepared and betrayed, the defending armies of young King Peter capitulated within ten days. As Peter and his top men fled to exile, Yugoslavia's foes swooped on the luckless country. Germany, Italy, Bulgaria, Hungary and Albania dismembered most of the territory; the remainder fell under the rule of collaborators.

But the vanquished struck back. Guerrilla bands soon organized large-scale resistance activities. Initially, in 1941 the communist-led Partisans and royalist Chetniks under Col. Draža Mihajlović agreed to join forces against the enemy. But it soon became apparent that they were too incompatible politically to cooperate. Evidence increased that Chetniks were assisting the Germans against the Partisans. When the Allies began dropping supplies in 1943, it was only to the Partisans' National Liberation Army, commanded by Tito. The triumphant uphill fight of the Partisans in pinning down tens of thousands of enemy troops and finally liberating their own country has been widely told. The price the Yugoslavs paid for their liberty was high—the loss of over 1,700,000 lives.

## A Republic Proclaimed

At the end of 1943, Tito was named marshal of Yugoslavia and president of the National Liberation Committee (a provisional government). As peacetime leader of a new Yugoslavia—proclaimed a socialist federal republic on November 29, 1945—he totally altered the course of his country's economic and political life. In 1948 Yugoslavia broke with Stalin, abandoning Soviet tutelage to create a distinctive brand of socialism based on worker management and self-governing communes. The vexing nationalities question was met by giving each of the six republics almost complete autonomy in its internal affairs. The foreign policy of non-alignment (of which Tito was a founder) catapulted Yugoslavia to an international significance far beyond its size or wealth. With the death of Tito in 1980, Yugoslavia turned to the task of consolidating the real-life achievement of the legendary national leader.

*Breaking through a grid of clouds, sunrays fan out over the calm sea.*

# Where to Go

## Split

Pop. 236,000

Now Dalmatia's fastest growing city, Split began nearly 17 centuries ago with a magnificent palace built for a retiring Roman emperor. Its eventful past is recorded in stone—in Corinthian capitals, Romanesque and Gothic windows and stately Renaissance façades. Yet the imposing setting in no way inhibits the lively, gregarious people of Split.

The city itself is stretched across a peninsula with harbours on either side—one mainly for pleasure craft; the other, Yugoslavia's second seaport. Above the red-tiled roofs of the old town rises the campanile of the cathedral. Behind, tall, new buildings glisten white against the blue haze of the Kozjak and Mosor mountains. Overlooking town and harbour, on the western tip of the peninsula, is wooded Marjan hill.

People wonder why Diocletian decided to build a palace here. According to tradition, he was born near neighbouring Salona and wanted to return here to spend his last years. Others hold that the ailing Diocletian sought relief in the sulphur springs just outside the palace walls (still used for cures). And there's also a story that the soil was particularly good for growing cabbages, the Roman emperor's hobby.

Whatever the reason, when Diocletian abdicated in A.D. 305, a palace that had taken ten years to build awaited him. After his death, it served as a residence for governors and exiled emperors. In the 7th century, when barbarian tribes devastated Salona, its inhabitants took refuge within the palace walls, partitioning off the vast imperial apartments for their more modest needs.

During the following centuries, Split recognized in turn the sovereignty of the Byzantine empire, the medieval Croatian state and the Croatian-Hungarian kings, retaining throughout considerable autonomy in municipal affairs. At the end of this period, Split again offered asylum, this time to Hungarian King Bela IV and his court, who fled before the Tartar hordes.

In 1420, the city came under Venetian dominion, but it still had to contend with the Turks, who controlled the surrounding area for the next three centuries. Forced to concentrate all its energies on defence,

Split declined. The Austrians took over in 1797 and, except for a brief Napoleonic interim, held on until the end of World War I.

Throughout all adversity, the people of Split have always been intensely independent, proud of any show of local spirit. In World War II, the city's most popular soccer team, almost to a man, joined Tito's Partisans.

Many a tourist has wandered through the narrow streets of Split looking for **Diocletian's Palace,** only to find out he was *in* it. Over the centuries, new buildings have been tacked on, inner walls torn down and arches walled up as practical or artistic considerations dictated. The city began within the massive walls and gradually grew beyond them.

So, before setting out, take a look at the palace layout. Towers guard the corners of the thick stone ramparts, while two main streets cross the pal-

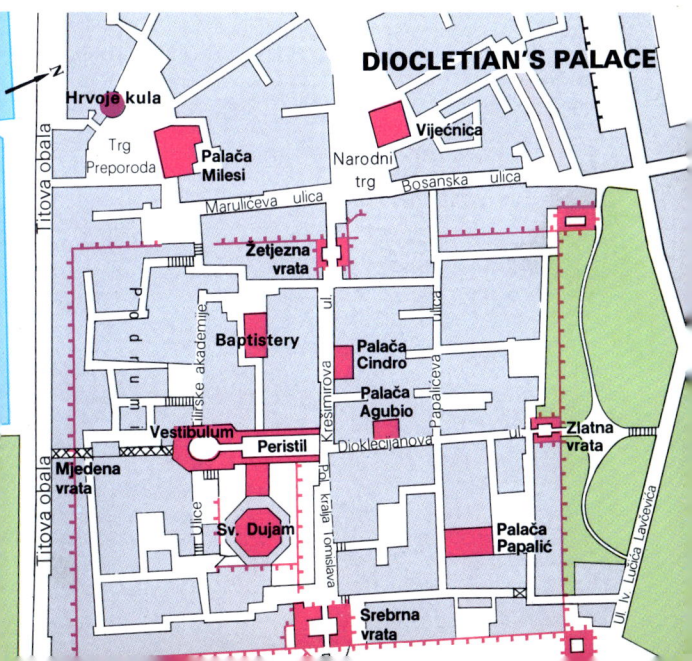

ace at right angles, leading to the four ancient gates—Golden *(Zlatna vrata)*, Silver *(Srebrna vrata)*, Bronze *(Mjedena vrata)* and Iron *(Zeljezna vrata)*. In the northern half of the complex lived the servants and legionaries; the emperor had his private apartments in the southern half. High above the seafront wall, an arched colonnade ran the length of the southern façade, providing a covered walkway for the imperial family—with a splendid view of the sea.

It's best to start your tour at the waterfront. The colonnade is just discernible above the shops now embedded in the palace walls. The spaces between the original free-standing columns have been filled in.

Halfway along, wedged between souvenir shops and travel agencies, is the Bronze Gate,

*You can sit down and have a drink right inside Diocletian's Palace.*

leading down to recently cleared **cellars** *(Podrumi)*. Deliciously cool in summer, the vaulted halls were directly below the imperial apartments, long since demolished. The thick walls indicate the dimensions of the emperor's quarters which were built on the same plan.

A flight of steps goes up to the **Peristyle** *(peristil)*, a courtyard that has defied destruction by time or man over the centuries. Immense Corinthian columns border the sunken pavement on three sides. The fourth side opens onto the intersection of the two main streets. The row of columns on the left was closed up by medieval houses. The arches of this freestanding arcade sprang directly from the columns, a daring departure that was crucial in the development of architecture.

Behind the stairs, a monumental portico leads to the circular, now domeless, **vestibule.** Here, visiting dignitaries used to cool their heels while waiting to be summoned to the imperial presence.

A black Egyptian sphynx, already 2,000 years old when the palace was erected, guards the entrance to the emperor's mausoleum, now the **Cathedral of St. Domnius** *(Sveti Dujam)*.

*A stroll through Split's open-air market titillates eye and palate.*

Climbing its steps, you pass through a medieval bell tower (fine view from the top). Built in stages from the 13th to the 17th century, it was finally restored late last century.

Twenty-four columns gird the octagonal mausoleum. The outside has not changed since Diocletian's time. The interior, on the other hand, has received contributions from virtually every era. The remarkable **carved wooden doors** by Andrija Buvina, illustrating scenes from the life of Christ, the hexagonal stone pulpit and Dalmatia's oldest choir stalls date from the 13th century. If you look closely at the stalls, you'll see a miniature relief showing the artist at work. Left of the high altar is a canopied Gothic shrine (1448) by Juraj Dalmatinac, one of the best-known Slav sculptors. Under a reclining St. Anastasius, a small panel depicts a particularly realistic rendition of the *Flagellation*.

As a reminder of the building's original purpose, images of Emperor Diocletian and his consort gaze down from medallions in the frieze below the dome.

Across the colonnaded court, an alley leads to a small temple, probably dedicated to Jupiter. All that remains is the inner sanctuary, which early Christians turned into a **baptistery.** On guard before its handsome portal is another sphinx of black granite, this one headless. The centre stone slab on the baptismal font (11th century) shows a medieval Croatian king seated on his throne. Behind the font is a bronze statue of **St. John the Baptist** by Ivan Meštrović. The rather stark interior is vaulted by an elaborate, coffered ceiling. Its flowers and fantastic figures stand out best when illuminated.

From the peristyle and its cluster of café tables, a wide thoroughfare with the original Roman paving takes you to the Silver Gate. Here the flower vendors' parasols make pinwheels of colour against the white stone. Through the gate and past the souvenir stalls,

*Flower stalls cluster around Silver Gate; in background, St. Domnius'.*

*Arcaded square makes a colourful backdrop for summer performances.*

you come to the open-air market, the busiest place in town from sun-up to midday.

The other two streets that branch out from the peristyle carry you a thousand years forward. You need no guide here, just time to enjoy contrasts. Behind a pair of Romanesque arches, a boutique has opened up. Geraniums spill over a medieval gallery, and a small child wheels his tricycle in a venerable columned courtyard. For all its architectural splendour, Split is still very much lived in.

Diocletian Street *(Dioklecijanova ulica)* leads to the **Golden Gate,** Krešimirova Street to the Iron Gate. Just off Diocletian Street is the Venetian

Gothic **palace of the Papalić family.** A flamboyant example of the work of Juraj Dalmatinac, it now serves as the city museum. The ground floor contains a fine collection of weapons from the 15th to the 18th century, Turkish and European small arms among others.

Outside the Golden Gate, you have a view of the whole north wall. It helps you appreciate the enormity of the palace and the strength of the stone walls that held back wave after wave of barbarians. Understandably, little remains of the original decoration. The small enclosure just inside the gateway, between the inner and outer walls, served as a checkpoint where travellers had to identify themselves.

Just outside the gate stands Meštrović's huge bronze **statue** of Bishop Gregory of Nin *(Grgur Ninski),* a controversial figure who defended both the early Croatian church and the Slavonic language.

Leaving the palace, the Iron Gate leads to National Square *(Narodni trg),* where young and old congregate in the early evening. You can hear the hum of spirited conversation a block away.

High above the gate is an unusual clock tower that tells time in Roman numerals. The triple-arched loggia opposite belongs to the old town hall, today an **ethnographic museum.** Its exhibits include costumes, lace, jewelry and some handcrafted items. (Look for the amusing carved whistles.)

Nearby Renaissance Square *(Trg Preporoda)* is dominated by the 15th-century Hrvoje Tower, part of the fortifications the Venetians built to hold off the Turks. In the middle of the square is the Meštrović statue of Marko Marulić (1450–1524), a Croatian poet who warned Europe of the Ottoman threat.

**Finding Your Way**

| | |
|---|---|
| *centar grada* | city centre |
| *crkva* | church |
| *kaštel* | castle |
| *kolodvor* | railway station |
| *muzej* | museum |
| *pjaca, placa,* | square |
| *plaža* | beach |
| *obala* | quay |
| *staza* | footpath |
| *trg* | square |
| *tržnica* | market |
| *tvrdjava* | fort |
| *ulica* | street |
| *vrata* | gate |
| *desno* | right |
| *levo* | left |
| *pravo* | straight ahead |

## From Shepherd to Sculptor

All over Dalmatia, you will see the powerful statues of Ivan Meštrović, Yugoslavia's best-known modern sculptor.

As a shepherd boy in a mountain village near Šibenik, he whittled figures in wood while tending his sheep. His natural talent was soon noticed, and he was apprenticed to a stonemason in Split. At the age of 16, Meštrović made his way to the Vienna Academy. Later, he worked in Paris, where he came under the influence of Auguste Rodin.

After World War II, Meštrović moved to the United States. He died, a naturalized American citizen, in Indiana in 1962.

Meštrović's heroic figures add a dramatic note to many a Yugoslav church, courtyard or museum. At the Meštrović Gallery in Split, you can see the full range of his work in wood, marble and bronze.

*Meštrović statue of 10th-century Croatian bishop, Gregory of Nin.*

The Milesi Palace, jutting out into the square, has a bookshop on the ground floor and the **Maritime Museum** *(Pomorski muzej)* upstairs (entrance around the corner). The copy of a 4,000-year-old pot fragment, unearthed on Hvar Island, bears the oldest picture of a sailing boat in Europe. In the model-ship collection, note the **liburna,** a swift Illyrian galley copied by the Romans. These ships were used against the navy of Antony and Cleopatra at Actium, contributing—it is claimed—to their defeat. A narrow passage alongside the Venetian tower leads back to the waterfront.

Split has several beaches— the best known is Bačvice. But for a change, especially with children, head for **Marjan,** the wooded hill where Diocletian hunted. Along the edge of the harbour, you pass arcaded Trg Republike, a memento from the Austrians. Farther along is the Franciscan church *(Sveti Frane)*. The climb up the Botićevo Šetalište steps to a terrace on Marjan hill will reward you with magnificent views of the city and of the islands. There's also a small zoo.

You can take a bus (No. 12) along the shore road to the **Meštrović Gallery** (see p. 76), formerly the sculptor's summer residence. Not far from here is a small castle *(Kaštelet)*. Its chapel, decorated by Meštrović, has wooden carvings illustrating the life of Christ. Nearby is the newly built **Muzej hrvatskih arheoloških spomenika** (on *Ognjena price*), featuring Croatian archaeological discoveries. At the tip of the

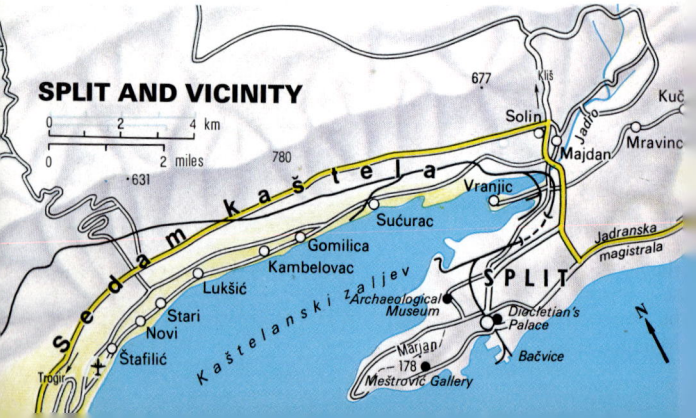

peninsula are the Oceanographic Institute and a small aquarium.

Another **Archaeological Museum** is located in the northern section of town on Zrinjsko-Frankopanska Street (see p. 76). It contains the finest pieces discovered in the Roman and Early Christian ruins at Salona.

While admiring "the memorials and the things of fame that do renown this town" — Split claims to be the Illyrian city of Shakespeare's *Twelfth Night* — you can collect personal impressions. Dally a while in a café over an *espresso* or *cappuccino*. The ebullient group at the next table is probably replaying last Sunday's soccer game or arguing about the merits of the city's water-polo team. Strollers greet friends in a flurry of handshakes and kisses on both cheeks, inquiring after health and reporting extensively on their own. The evening *korzo*, or promenade, will give them a chance to catch up on gossip. After nightfall, you may hear the sound of men's voices joining in close harmony: sitting in a café or on some stone steps, they sing of romance, of the sea and especially of their beloved Split and its landmark, Marjan.

*Roman ruins for archaeology buffs, beetles and bugs for the small fry.*

## Excursions from Split

One popular day trip for tourists takes in the ruins of ancient **Salona** (near SOLIN, 5 km. to the northeast). Soon after leaving Split, the arches of a Roman aqueduct loom into view. Originally built to supply the emperor's palace and restored in the 19th century, the aqueduct still carries water into Split from the Jadro River.

The Romans had already tapped this source for Salona,

the most important town in Roman Dalmatia in Diocletian's time. It had an arena, theatre, temples and baths. In a burst of early Christian fervour, 30 churches and basilicas were added. However, the marauding Avars and Slavs put the townspeople to flight in 614. For centuries after, the abandoned site was a huge quarry of stone, with free building material for the taking.

Scattered over a wide slope amid the foundations of basilicas lie tilted sarcophagi, broken columns, fragments of stone doorways. The archaeologist who excavated this site incorporated some of these relics in the walls of his summer cottage, an eccentric idea that's rather symbolic of the fate of the town.

The fortress of **Klis** (9 km. from Split) is another destination for excursions. Guarding a pass between the Kozjak and Mosor mountains, the stronghold was the scene of a heroic battle in 1537. Petar Kružić led his band of Uskoks from Senj in a valiant but unsuccessful attempt to relieve the fort under siege by the Turks. Kružić lost his life in the fighting.

Wild and fearless on land and on sea, the Uskoks were originally fugitives from the Turkish-held territories. They harried both Turkish and Venetian shipping, and their exploits are celebrated in Croatian folk ballads. Several English adventurers are known to have sailed with them.

The climb to the fortress is worth the effort. Three rings of walls, added by the Turks, mount to the crest of the hill. The Turks also put up a mosque (a rarity in these parts), but its minaret was removed when it became a Christian church. A stroll along the ramparts affords marvellous views of the rugged mountains, Split and the islands offshore.

In August, the town of SINJ (34 km. from Split) has a spectacular **tournament** *(Sinjska alka),* commemorating another encounter with the Turks. This time the natives fared better. For more than 250 years, colourfully costumed descendants of those staunch men have competed in an annual contest of marksmanship. One by one, they gallop by, thrusting their lances at the heart of a suspended ring *(alka),* symbol of the stirrup of the unhorsed Turkish pasha (see p. 74).

*Klis fortress, scene of heroic battle between the Turks and Uskoks.*

Also in mid-summer, nearby VRLIKA holds a traditional festival called the *dernek*. This draws crowds of visitors and costumed country folk, each eyeing the other with curiosity. Holiday best for the men consists of tassled red caps and fancifully embroidered vests studded with metal knobs. To their own lavish costumes, the women add heavy necklaces of metal coins. These jingle to the rhythm of an exciting folk dance performed for the occasion.

*Rural life moves slowly, a restful change from a car-dominated world.*

# North of Split

Scattered along the crescent of a wide bay are the SEDAM KAŠTELA (Seven Castles), a string of villages that developed around the fortified holdings of medieval landlords. Ancient stone houses cluster about a crenellated fort or form a tight knot at the water's edge. A resort area since the 19th century, summer houses line the beaches of pebble and sand shaded by pines. The brief, mild winters—almond trees flower in February—leave many months for pleasant holidays.

To reach the seven villages— KAŠTEL SUĆURAC, KAŠTEL GOMILICA, KAŠTEL KAMBELOVAC, KAŠTEL LUKŠIĆ, KAŠTEL STARI, KAŠTEL NOVI and KAŠTEL ŠTAFILIĆ—you leave the Adriatic Highway at Solin and take an older road that runs near the sea.

For the feel of the past, don't miss the ancient town of **Trogir** (27 km. from Split), rising out of the sea on an island of its own. One bridge connects it with the mainland, another to an outlying island that shelters it from the open sea. As you enter, Trogir draws you immediately into a web of intertwining streets with patterns of cubes and steps, broken by the

curves of vaulted passageways.

The first here, after the goats, were Greeks of the 3rd century B.C. They named their new colony after the grazing herd. One vestige of these early settlers is a bas-relief, now in the Benedictine convent, of the Greek god of opportunity. A very slippery fellow, he shaved the back of his head so that once he got past you there was little chance of catching him again.

Trogir, like Split, opened her gates to the refugees from Salona and also to Hungarian King Bela IV. The townspeople gallantly refused to turn the king over to the Tartars, who, fortunately, withdrew as suddenly as they had come. In those turbulent times, Trogir sought to maintain autonomy by diplomacy and all other means.

But in 1420, after four days of heavy bombardment, the town fell to Venice. The Venetians stayed on for four centuries, relinquishing their hold only to the Austrians in 1797. The attractive belvedere at the western end of the island is a legacy of the Napoleonic occupation (1806–14).

The town's narrow streets, packed with medieval houses of weathered stone, lead to the **cathedral** on the main square. It took three centuries to build. Though officially dedicated to St. Lawrence *(Sveti Lovrijenac),* popular sentiment gives it to St. John, the patron saint of Trogir. The campanile was built in various stages, accounting for the mixed architectural styles. The first part (1240) had to be rebuilt 200 years later after Venetian bombardment.

The magnificent Romanesque **main portal** is the work of a local sculptor, who confidently inscribed the following in Latin: "Radovan, the mos excellent in his art, as the statues and reliefs show..." On either side of the doorway stand Adam and Eve with thick-maned lions at their feet. The rich detail includes figures of apostles and other saints, real and mythical beasts and a fascinating series showing the daily life of medieval peasants.

The carvings also illustrate such familiar biblical stories as the Nativity, the three kings and the Last Supper.

Inside the cathedral, a ciborium, one of the oldest in Dalmatia, forms a striking two-storey canopy over the main altar. The pulpit, elevated on eight slender columns, dates

*Left: the loquacious Yugoslavs always enjoy a friendly exchange; below: the red rooftops of Trogir, originally settled by the Greeks.*

back to the 13th century. The beautifully carved Gothic **choir stalls** merit a close look.

For a Renaissance highlight, pause at the **chapel of St. John Orsini,** where robust stone cherubs playfully thrust torches through half-open doors. More spiritual in cast are the elaborately draped figures of Christ, Mary and some of the apostles and other saints in the niches above. A glance upwards at the coffered ceiling will tell you that Nicholas of Florence, the artist responsible for most of the work in this chapel, was impressed by the beauty of Jupiter's Temple in Split.

The sacristy contains some treasures: paintings of *John the Baptist* and *St. Jerome* by Gentile Bellini, a silver ewer presented by Elizabeth of Hungary (born in Trogir), a hood embroidered with gold and pearls which may have belonged to King Bela IV and a delicate, inlaid wardrobe.

Out in the main square, look for two sets of triple Gothic windows, one above the other. This is the façade of the **Ćipiko Palace,** probably the work of Nicholas of Florence. A member of the Ćipiko family invited the sculptor to Trogir; another family member commanded Trogir's galley in the battle of Lepanto (1571). Inside the palace, you'll find a wooden cock, a figurehead from the prow of a Turkish ship captured in the battle.

The column-fronted **loggia** (15th century) served as a court-house; the judge's bench and table are still in place. For the edification of both magistrate and accused, an Allegory of Justice, also by Nicholas of Florence, adorns the wall above. The damaged central portion once held a winged lion, a memento of Venetian rule that was blown off in an anti-Italian demonstration in 1932. A relief by Meštrović honours Bishop Petar Berislavić of Trogir, who lost his life fighting the Turks.

Before walking out on the waterfront, stop at the Benedictine convent for a look at the Greek **bas-relief** of the slippery god of luck. In the wall of the cloisters is an even older Greek relic: an inscription from the 3rd century B.C.

A stroll along the quay facing the island of Čiovo takes you past a smaller loggia where disembarking travellers could stay overnight until the town gates opened. This gate and the adjoining dungeon formed part of the original fortifications, removed in a 19th-century town-planning effort.

The palm-lined quay comes

*Souvenir of medieval elegance — the Gothic façade of Čipiko Palace.*

abruptly to an end at the sturdy **Fortress of Kamerlengo,** built in the 15th century to protect Venetian shipping from attacks by pirates and Turks. Now outdoor films and fashion shows are presented here. Past a pebble beach and the belvedere where the French Marshal Marmont is supposed to have enjoyed a game of cards, the Fort of St. Mark watches over a few rowing-boats.

The coastal road continues along the shore for a while and then swings away into a rugged, arid region. This is part of the *karst,* a belt of porous limestone stretching the length of the Yugoslav Adriatic coast. In the past, every hollow where a little soil collected was cultivated assiduously: hills were carved into terraces supporting a few vines, a clump of olive or fig trees. However, since entertaining tourists has proved to be a much easier way of earning a living, this painstaking method of agriculture has been largely abandoned.

Jutting out to sea is PRIMOŠTEN (31 km. from Trogir), an island settled and fortified in the 16th century by refugees from Turkish areas. Instead of the present causeway, a drawbridge connected the stronghold with the mainland. Every morning, the islanders crossed the bridge to the mainland; every evening, drums summoned them back before the bridge was drawn up securely for the night. Now, if you hear drums, they carry the beat of rock and roll — from the dance bands of the nearby hotels.

The neighbouring countryside is covered with a checkerboard of miniature vineyards. The criss-crossing walls of stone leave barely enough room for a half-dozen vines to take

35

*Spread on racks over the water, figs are left to dry out in sun.*

root, yet the grapes grown on these slopes yield wine noted for its delicate bouquet.

The shore road winds north following the rocks in their unending battle with the sea. Offshore you can see the first of the hundred or so islands that make up the Šibenik archipelago. Closest is the low-lying islet of KRAPANJ, first settled (1436) by Franciscan monks, then by others seeking island safety. In the 18th century the men learned to dive for sponges, leaving the women to till the fields on the mainland. You can still see the women rowing over, a donkey and farm tools loaded on the boat. Whether you cross over to the island to swim or to visit a wine-cellar, don't pass up a chance to see the museum at the Franciscan monastery. Sponges, coral and amphoras are on view along with a 16th-century *Last Supper* by Francesco da Santacroce.

### Šibenik
Pop. 37,000
*(Split, 88 km.)*

The best way to come into Šibenik is by sea, slipping past the steep grey cliffs into a wide lagoon. Opposite, the red-tiled roofs of the town climb the wooded slopes. Three fortresses still tower over the hilltops. The harbour, almost completely enclosed, is actually a widened bend in the Krka River which forces its way to sea through the narrow channel.

Šibenik's almost impregnable position did not save her from disaster. Siege, fire, plague and bombardment have all taken their toll. The town is first mentioned in connection with a Croatian assembly held here in 1066. In the next century, the Croatian-Hungarian kings gave Šibenik a charter, granting certain local privileges. Even after the Venetians took over (1412), the townspeople managed to hold on to some of these rights.

In the 16th century the plague struck: barely one-sixth of the population of 10,000 survived. The Turks tried to take the town a number of times, but their assaults were repulsed from the formidable hill fortresses. In 1797 the Austrians moved in, remaining until the end of World War I. World War II meant four more years of occupation and heavy bombing. Since then, Šibenik's fortunes have clearly changed: its vigorous industrial growth and burgeoning tourist trade have completely transformed the region.

Fortunately, the old quarter has changed very little in the past 1,000 years. Centuries of calamity forced the people to use durable building materials, resistant to fire, water and cannon balls. Sturdy houses of stone rise in tiers, and staircases scale the steep hill from the waterfront to the Fort of St. Anne on the craggy summit.

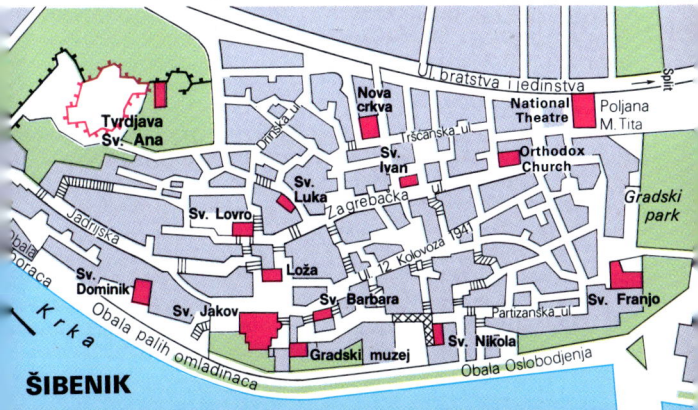

Before exploring this labyrinth of sinuous alleyways, visit the city's finest monument, the **Cathedral of St. James** *(Sveti Jakov)*. Its construction in the 15th and 16th centuries was beset by so many financial difficulties that notaries were required by law to remind any citizen drawing up a will to bequeath funds for the cathedral.

In front of the church stands Meštrović's statue of Juraj Dalmatinac, the artist who can be credited with the cathedral's best features. An intriguing—and unusual—**frieze** by Dalmatinac decorates the outer walls of the apses. It comprises over 70 heads of stone: citizens, one story has it, who neglected to donate to the cathedral. Several may represent faces of the builders.

You enter the cathedral by a side portal, flanked by lions and the Romanesque figures of Adam and Eve. (Bronze doors are a recent addition.) Inside, slender Gothic columns separate the aisles from the spacious nave, which is bathed in iridescent light from the stained-glass window overhead. Above each arcade runs a double row of acanthus leaves blowing in the wind, a motif Juraj repeated wherever he worked. After his death, Nicholas of Florence took over, completing the upper portion of the interior and choir area. Note the unique, barrel-vaulted roof, constructed entirely of huge slabs of stone.

Saving the best for last: to the right of the choir and down a few steps, you come to the

**Signature in Stone**
Juraj Dalmatinac was a man of many names—Juraj Šibenčanin, Giorgio Orsini or Georgius Dalmaticus, as he signed his work—and of many talents—sculptor, architect and town planner.

Little is known of his life. A native of Zadar, Dalmatinac received his training in Venice about the time the Doge's Palace was being built. He worked in Split, Dubrovnik, Pag, Ancona, Rimini and Ravenna, designing palaces, portals, chapels and statues. He often set up workshops to train apprentices. Stonework called for lots of help.

By 1441, his reputation led the notables of Šibenik to ask him to complete their cathedral. This was to be his masterpiece. Like his other work, the cathedral bears his personal stamp—a vigourous style and a new note of realism.

*Dalmatinac's masterpiece, Sveti Jakov Cathedral, with its curious frieze of stone-sculpted portraits.*

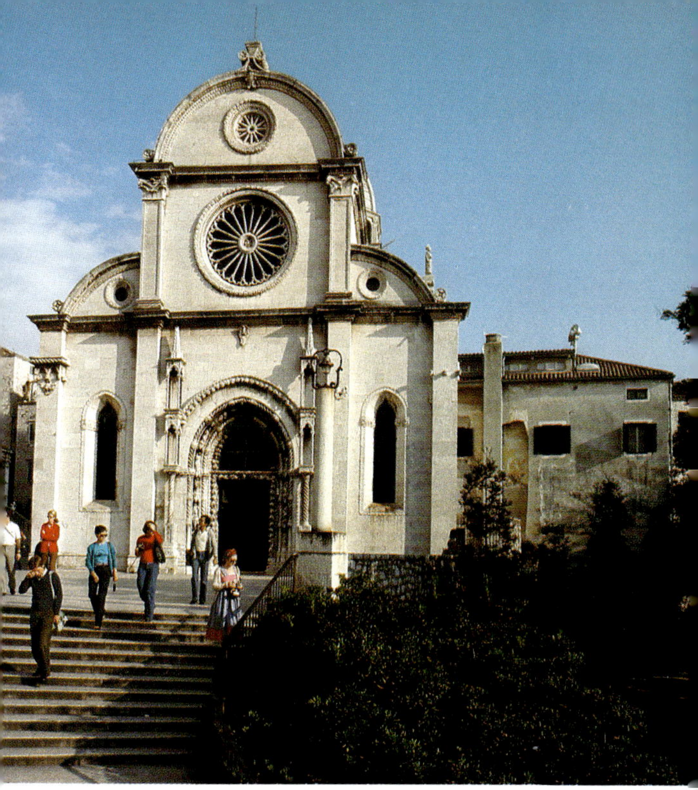
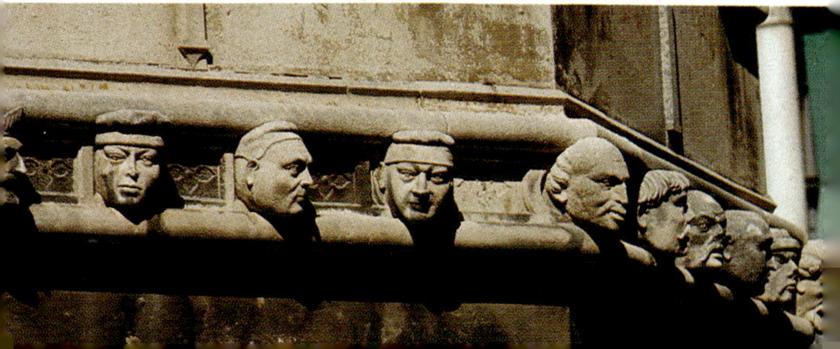

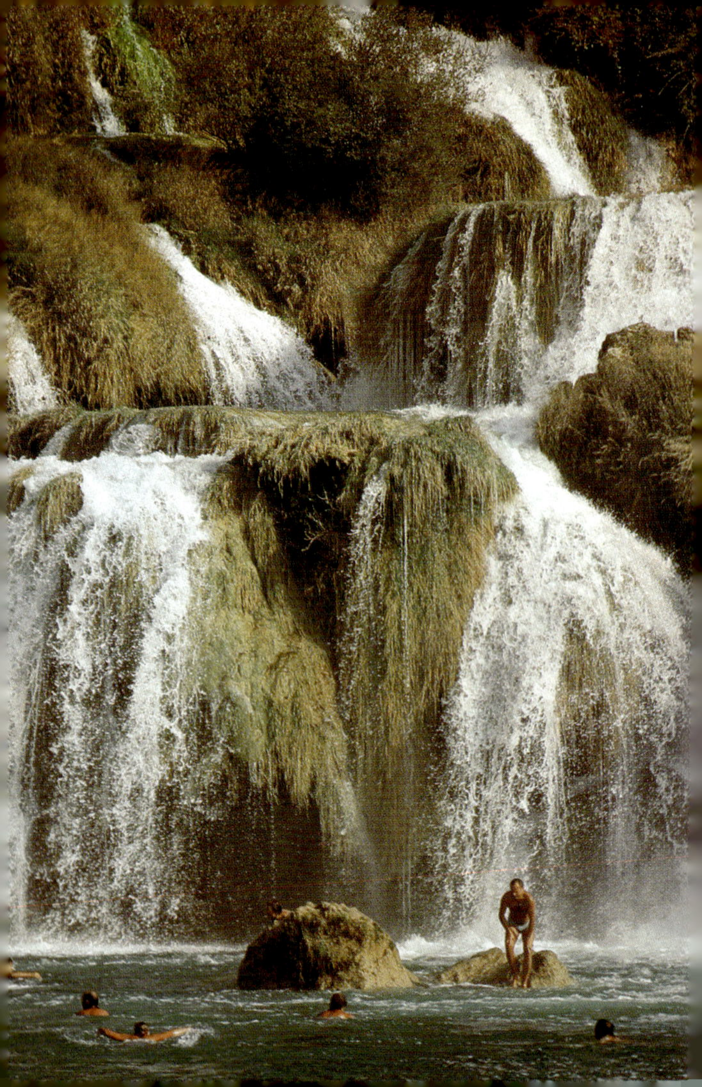

**baptistery.** Largely the work of Dalmatinac, this is a tiny chamber of ribbed conches, converging crescents and Gothic tracery. A delightful trio of cherubs support the baptismal font.

In the square, café tables stand in the shade of the arcaded city loggia, often used as a backdrop for summer performances. For archaeology buffs, the **Town Museum** *(Gradski muzej)*, former residence of the Venetian administrator, has a collection of neolithic artefacts recently unearthed in the vicinity. Other exhibits present the work of Juraj Dalmatinac (see p. 77).

Roam around the **old quarter** any time of day. First thing in the morning you may catch a housewife out in front of her house giving the paving stones a thorough sweeping, a custom that is, sadly, dying out. Any of a dozen old churches may open its doors for morning mass, often your only opportunity to see the interior. There's even an Orthodox church *(Uspenje Bogorodice)*, rare in these parts, with an attractive twin-balconied bell tower. Steep steps and twisting streets lead up to the Fort of St. Anne *(Tvrdjava Sveta Ana)* and the old cemetery (rows of vaults built right into the hillside). You'll be rewarded with a splendid view.

At siesta hour the streets become deserted, filling up again as evening approaches. This is the time to join strollers along the main street *(Ulica 12 kolovoza 1941)* leading up to the National Theatre and the new town square. A very leisurely pace is in order. Inspect the souvenir shops for gifts to take home, stop at a café until the smell of sizzling meat lures you into a garden restaurant.

There's a marvellous choice of side trips from Šibenik. Along the spectacular upper courses of the Krka River, water thunders over travertine barriers in cascades that freshen the summer air. A favourite picnic spot, the **Krka Falls** *(Skradinski buk)* can be reached by boat, bus or car (17 km.). In calmer waters, the island of VISOVAC harbours a Franciscan monastery. Further upstream, past other falls, an old Orthodox monastery *(Arhandjelovac)* stands by the river.

For nautical adventure, take a motor launch from Šibenik

*The adventure of a cool plunge under the thundering Krka Falls.*

and sail through the winding channel, past Jadrija beach, to the islands. The first port of call is ZLARIN, whose inhabitants once earned their living by diving for coral and fashioning it into jewelry. Today only one workshop remains. The women still wear an attractive costume, so take along your camera.

The island of PRVIĆ contains the grave of historian, physicist and inventor Faust Vrančić. His book *Machinae Novae* (1605) has one of the earliest descriptions of a parachute. Incidentally, this Padua-educated scholar may have been an early feminist: he also wrote *The Lives of Some Outstanding Women*.

About a hundred more islands and islets, few of them inhabited, extend to the west.

Heading north, the coastal road crosses the single-span bridge over the Krka. The fork for VODICE (15 km. from Šibenik) leads to a burgeoning resort area. The village itself, named after the freshwater springs tapped by some 1,000 wells, lies on a shallow bay. Hotels and camping sites are scattered around the bay, pleasantly located in pine woods and close to the beaches.

The road continues inland until the turn-off for Murter. Connected to the mainland by a bridge, MURTER is an island of low-spreading hills covered with scrub and sparse pine — for the moment still off the tourist track. At the north-west end are the towns of BETINA, known for its seaworthy boats, and MURTER, the largest settlement (33 km. from Šibenik). Several sandy coves attract the summer visitors who normally stay with a local farmer or fisherman, often eating at his table. Since the villagers own most of the Kornati Islands, many excursions start here.

For spectacular seascapes, do take a boat trip to the KORNATI ISLANDS, over a hundred barren humps protruding from the crystal-clear sea. Some of them have rather odd names — like Babina guzica, Grandma's Backside — supposedly invented by the fun-loving fishermen who accompanied Austrian map-makers. On the seaward side, cliffs rise straight from the water; pockets, sheltered from the abrasive, salt-laden winds, conceal patches of vegetation and traces of homes now abandoned. Fish abound. In the surrounding waters, the rocks are worn into crevices and niches inhabited by coral, shellfish and a myriad of other marine organisms. You'll find marvellous cruising, bathing, fishing and scuba-diving. If you want to rough it, try a "Robinson Crusoe" holiday. You stay in a fisherman's hut on one of these deserted islands—but with your daily supply of groceries, mail and newspapers delivered by boat.

Back on the mainland, the coastal road follows a narrow strip of land that separates the long lake of VRANA *(Vransko jezero)* from the sea. In Roman days, an aqueduct carried fresh water over 30 kilometres to Zadar. Today a canal dug across the isthmus to the sea has made the lake water brackish. But it's still good for

*For a complete change, stay at a fisherman's home or camp out on one of Kornati's deserted islands.*

*Country fairs draw crowds looking for a bargain or just a good time.*

fishing (carp, mullet, eel) and duck hunting.

PAKOŠTANE and CRVENA LUKA are developing into holiday playgrounds where you can interrupt idle sun-tanning with a bit of water-skiing or a speedboat or kayak outing.

Stretching across a small peninsula and inland, BIOGRAD NA MORU (white-city-by-the sea, 44 km. from Šibenik) is an old hand at entertaining visitors. Its popular beach twists into a sandy cove, edged by dense pine woods that provide welcome shade for picnickers and campers.

You'll find little evidence nowadays that ten centuries back Biograd was a royal town, residence of the medieval Croatian kings. When Croatia and Hungary were united under a single crown in 1102, Koloman travelled to Biograd for his coronation. But shortly after, in a demonstration of power, the Venetian doge had the town levelled to its foundations. Destroyed again by the Turks in the 17th century, Biograd never recovered.

On the 10th of the month, tourists flock to the fair at BENKOVAC, 24 kilometres inland. Countryfolk from the surrounding villages bring farm produce and handiwork to sell. If you're looking for a souvenir, the most interesting items are woodcarvings and handwoven bags. Don't forget to bargain. Whole lambs roasting on the spit and an abundance of local wines add to the festive spirit.

## Zadar
Pop. 60,000
*(Split, 161 km.)*

Well situated on an important sailing route to the Near East, ancient Zadar — once the capital of Dalmatia — is bounded on three sides by the sea. Grey defensive walls still line the narrow harbour that's almost closed off by a breakwater. From the modern town, a footbridge spanning the harbour leads to the fortifications. Beyond lies old Zadar, a city coveted, conquered and rebuilt time and again. The most recent devastation occurred during World War II, when bombs flattened whole blocks of medieval buildings.

Inhabited since Illyrian times, Zadar is first mentioned in connection with a Greek victory in the 4th century B.C.

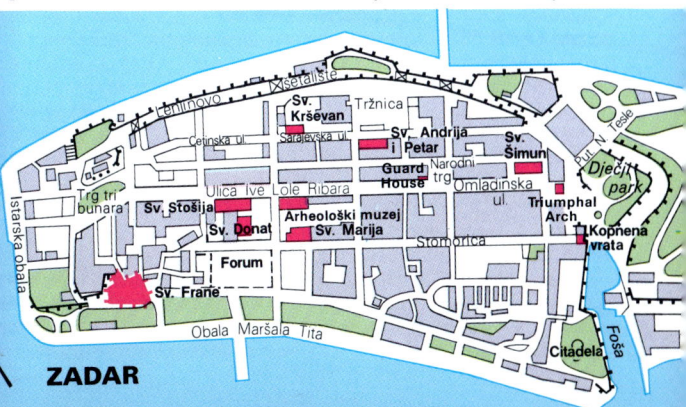

Roman colonists arrived in the 1st century B.C. and laid out the usual grid of streets with a magnificent forum in the centre. After the division of the Roman empire, Zadar became the seat of the Byzantine governor.

The town's strategic importance was recognized very early: between the 8th and 16th centuries it changed hands 30 times. After a brief period under Charlemagne, three powers—Venice, Croatia and later Hungary-Croatia—vied for control. In 1202, the wily Venetian doge induced the knights of the Fourth Crusade to sack Zadar in exchange for ships to the Holy Land.

Later, Venice made a deal with her Adriatic rival, Ladislaus of Naples, paying 100,000 ducats for rights in Dalmatia. Venetian military engineers turned Zadar into a formidable stronghold: a massive fortress straddled the neck of land linking town and mainland. Existing moats were converted into reservoirs, and new ones were excavated on either side of the fortress—a system of defence the Turks found impregnable. Following the Venetians, the Austrians, then the Italians, took over. Zadar didn't become part of Yugoslavia until after World War II.

If you start out to explore Zadar in the early evening, just follow the crowd flowing into the old town from the footbridge. You'll soon find yourself on National Square *(Narodni trg)*. It's a good place to get your bearings and easy to find again because of the 16th-century **Guard House** with its clock tower. The Guard House now serves as the Ethnographic Museum, featuring a colourful collection of peasant costumes. Across the square is the town loggia, formerly a law court.

Taking the street named after partisan hero Ivo Lola Ribar—thronged at *korzo* time—you come to an open area strewn with fragments of the Roman forum. Dominating this space is a massive, circular church dedicated to **St. Donatus** *(Sveti Donat),* an imposing structure from the early 9th century. Entire columns and stone slabs from the forum were incorporated in St. Donatus'—and indeed in most of the town's other churches. The edifice, empty now, is sometimes used for summer concerts.

As you pick your way between the foundations in front of the church, look for half a dozen box-shaped walls. These were the *tabernae*, or shops, in the Roman forum that extended from this point under and beyond the church and adjoining buildings. Close by is a tall Roman column, used as a pillory in the Middle Ages. The chain still hangs from it.

The new Archaeological Museum boasts a vast collection of Roman and early Croatian antiquities. Next to it is St. Mary's *(Sveta Marija)*, which belongs to a chapter of Benedictine nuns founded by a Croatian noblewoman in the 11th century. Priceless ecclesiastical vessels known as the Silver and Gold of Zadar are kept here.

A splendid Romanesque façade with rows of blind arcades and two rose windows graces the **Cathedral of St. Anastasia** *(Sveta Stošija)*, built in the 12th and 13th centuries on the site of an earlier church. In-

*The chronicles of ill-fated Zadar begin at the ruins of a Roman forum.*

side, look for the 9th-century marble sarcophagus of St. Anastasia in the left apse. The damaged frescoes on the wall above depict Christ and, curiously enough, St. Thomas à Becket.

See, too, the Gothic **choir stalls** before the main altar, the 14th-century canopy above it and the marble seats in the apse behind, dating from the earlier Byzantine church.

Not far from here is the Franciscan monastery *(Sveti Frane),* reconstructed several times. Though uninteresting architecturally, the 13th-century church does possess some valuable paintings: a *St. Francis of Assisi* by Palma Giovane and, in its treasury, a collection of illuminated psalters, eucharistic vessels and early printed books. St. Francis himself is supposed to have visited Zadar in 1219.

Other churches in the area worth visiting include the 12th-century church of **St. Chrysogonus** *(Sveti Krševan),* dedicated to the patron saint of Zadar (see the lovely arcading on the main apse), and two very small and very old churches on Sarajevska Street, connected by a passageway. Different parts of the walls date from the 6th to the 9th centuries. You enter St. Andrew's *(Sveti Andrija)* first and then step through a door in the apse into the church of St. Peter the Old *(Sveti Petar Stari).* The latter,

*Zadar's produce vendors scarcely notice the shadows of antiquity.*

distinguished by an unusual two-aisled nave, contains stones, columns and altars taken from the forum.

An important feature of life in Zadar is the **market-place,** fortunately not yet put out of business by supermarkets. Here kerchiefed peasant women weigh out garden-fresh fruits and vegetables—cherries, peaches, beans, tomatoes, whatever happens to be in season. The produce is sold from dawn to midday, when the farmers pack up their baskets and go home. Dinars from the sale of eggs, a small round of hard cheese and a couple of chickens often find their way into the till of the nearest dry-goods store. You may want to pause at the souvenir stalls, a recent addition to markets in the holiday region.

Starting back in Narodni trg, a second loop in our walking tour leads down Omladinska Street to the church of St. Simeon *(Sveti Šimun).* Pilgrims on their way to the Holy Land used to stop in Zadar to see its greatest treasure, a **sarcophagus** of wrought silver. This masterpiece of 14th-century craftsmanship holds the remains of St. Simeon, who, legend relates, was left unidentified in the town cemetery after a shipwreck. Credited with miraculous powers, the saint's relics attracted many pilgrims, among them the future King Henry IV of England.

Past a column, taken from the forum, and what used to be a Roman triumphal arch, you arrive at a tall 13th-century tower *(Bablja kula)*—splendid view from the top. With the adjoining wall, it's all that has survived of the early medieval fortifications. Five attractive wells were placed behind the tower by the Venetians when they ringed the town with new bastions and converted the old moat into a reservoir. The children's park, just up the steps, was once a fortress.

The great 16th-century Land Gate *(Kopnena vrata)* bears a somewhat damaged winged lion of St. Mark, flanked by the coats-of-arms of the Venetian officials who built the gate. The mounted figure on the keystone is Zadar's St. Chrysogonus.

In the charming, little port of Foša below, small craft bob up and down at their moorings. The large park beyond occupies the site of the city's outer line of defence against the Turks.

The neighbourhood near the Land Gate, spared by the bombs of World War II, has retained much of its medieval

*Church of Sveti Križ at Nin, once the capital of medieval Croatia.*

aspect. In their day, these towns probably held little of the charm that enchants us today. Life was brief and, most assuredly, uncomfortable. But this needn't keep us from admiring the graceful lines of a Gothic window or portal or peering into delightful arcaded courtyards.

If you have time for strolling, a tree-shaded promenade runs along the top ramparts. On the busy waterfront below, tanned fishermen scour their boats while excursionists crowd into the ferry.

As a holiday region, Zadar has bounded ahead in recent years. Like many Yugoslav resorts, a good part of the hotels are located outside the populated urban area. A few minutes from Zadar, there's a sandy beach on the wooded promontory of BORIK, where guests can sun, swim or build sand castles for a change.

50

A further 15 kilometres along the coast is NIN, only a fishing village today but interesting because of its connection with the early Croatian kings. Those were the days when entire royal courts—king, queen, clergy, courtiers—moved around constantly from one town of the realm to another. Capital of medieval Croatia, Nin was also seat of the bishopric. A powerful statue by Meštrović (original in Split, copy in Nin) portrays Gregory *(Grgur)*, best known of the bishops. He championed the use of the Slavonic language in the church's liturgy.

History dealt so harshly with Nin that it holds little interest for anyone but archaeologists. Illyrian pottery, the foundations of Roman temples and medieval stonework have been unearthed at scattered sites. One thing that has survived is the small church of the Holy Cross *(Sveti Križ)*, its 9th-century exterior an attractive miniature of early Croatian architecture.

Driving east across the fertile plains that made the region as prosperous as it was difficult to defend, the first glimpse of water will be the landlocked SEA OF NOVIGRAD *(Novigradsko more)*. This cuts deep into the rugged interior—a highlight of boat trips from Zadar or nearby resorts.

A paved road skirting the rocky shore spirals down to NOVIGRAD town (40 km. from Zadar), hidden in a delightful, pine-fringed cove. Overlooking the town is a 13th-century fort where the final scenes of a royal tragedy were played out. Queen Elizabeth of Hungary was held prisoner here, 1386–87, during a conflict over succession to the throne and eventually executed.

On the opposite shore is the entrance to the starkly beautiful canyon of the Žrmanja River. Boat excursions run upstream to the ancient settlement of OBROVAC. Novigrad Sea connects with another inland body of water, the SEA OF KARIN, its barren shores relieved only by a reforestation project, shading a small colony of summer cottages. From Obrovac, continue inland through a lunar countryside to **Plitvice National Park,** 75-square miles of magnificent unspoilt woodland.

This spectacular natural attraction consists of 16 lakes, cascading into one another in a series of waterfalls. The highest lake *(Prošćansko jezero)* is 2,087 feet above sea level; the lowest *(Novakovića brod)* 1,650 feet. The lake water then thunders over the Sastavci falls to form the River Korana. Kozjak, the largest lake, has several attractive hotels, bungalows and a camping site on its wooded shores. Bathing, boating and trout-fishing (with a permit) are allowed in some areas. Amateur geologists will have a marvellous time inspecting rare travertine formations, numerous caves and other natural phenomena. The entrance ticket comes with a map indicating various walks and vantage points.

For a rest from holiday traffic on the main coastal road, bear left at the small fishing village of POSEDARIJE on Novigrad Sea, and head for the island of PAG, recently connected with the mainland by a new bridge. Crossing over, you have a breath-taking view of the mainland side of the island — rocky, waterless, windswept and most uninviting. Yet Pag once supported large Roman communities, and in medieval times rival powers fought for possession of what appears to be a massive pile of rock.

To solve this puzzle, look for brown specks scattered over the stony slopes. These turn out to be flocks of sheep, a remnant of the thousands that once cropped the now sparse grass. From their milk a sharp, highly prized cheese *(Paški sir)* is made. Another industry peculiar to the island, and unfortunately dying out, is the making of delicate, intricately worked lace. It was once shipped directly to the imperial court at Vienna. Near the town of Pag, the road follows the edge of ancient salt beds, the third and greatest source of income.

PAG town lies on a shallow,

*Novigrad's long waterfront curves around a romantic hideaway cove.*

protected bay, a site chosen in the 15th century when the old settlement was abandoned. The plans for the new town, for the prince's palace *(Kneževa palača)* and the unfinished bishop's palace are attributed to the Slav sculptor Juraj Dalmatinac. The parish church *(Uznesenje Marijino)* also warrants a visit: the tympanum above the main portal depicts the Virgin Mary sheltering the townspeople within her cloak. The women shown are wearing the typical island head-dress. Another attraction for summer visitors is the sandy beach that follows the whole crescent of the bay. Facilities for tourists are limited, though easy access may soon change this.

A modern asphalt-surfaced road now takes you all the way to NOVALJA, which has many Roman ruins and several good beaches. After a stroll around this quiet little town, with a glance at the stall vendors' wares, most sightseers turn back. Few venture onto the rough gravel track that runs to the end of the island and the village of LUN.

Just off Zadar's coastland the peaks and ridges of a sunken mountain range rise from the sea in a double strand of islands, over 200 of them, most uninhabited and wonderful for fishing and bathing. New tourist facilities are being developed to meet the growing demand for a quiet island holiday. After a few days in a snug fishing village, the cares of the world seem comfortably remote.

Directly opposite Zadar is UGLJAN, nearest and most visited island. The side facing the mainland is wooded and fertile with several villages in picturesque coves. As the shore weaves in and out, walkers constantly find themselves tempted to round one more point. The ruined 13th-century fortress of St. Michael *(Sveti Mihovil)* commands superb views; on a clear day, you can see as far as Italy.

The islands of Iž, the only place in northern Dalmatia where pottery is made, and DUGI OTOK (Long Island) also offer idyllic settings for lazing in the sun. The big event of the day here is going down to the waterfront and watching the steamer from the mainland come in.

*Only sheep can find enough to eat on stony slopes of Pag; below: a neighbourhood meeting place.*

# South of Split

After crossing a heavily built-up area south-east of Split, the Adriatic Highway swings towards the sea. Vineyards, peach orchards and walled vegetable plots dot the stony slopes. Down by the shore, where one village runs into the next, sandy beaches bring in a lively summer trade.

Snuggling against a steep mountain ridge by the Cetina River is **Omiš** (26 km. from Split), for centuries a corsair stronghold. The marauding bands based here harried the richly laden merchantmen sailing the Adriatic. On the grey, craggy rocks above rises a ruined medieval fort and a thousand feet higher (not visible from below) the remains of a huge fortress.

Explore the old quarter just across the low bridge. The ancient stone houses of decidedly modest origin are brightened by rows of blue and green wooden shutters. An annual contest of Dalmatian choral groups takes place in the square near the 17th-century parish church. Next to the clock tower is a 16th-century chapel dedicated to the Holy Spirit *(Sveti Duh)*; a painting by Palma the Younger hangs over the altar. The climb up to the fort is recommended only to the sure-footed.

The quay by the river is aptly named after the pirates *(Obala gusara)*. This is the starting point for boat-trips up through the beautiful gorge, the pirates' escape route, to an old stone mill converted into a restaurant.

For some spectacular scenery and a good view of the gorge, drive back across the bridge and take the new asphalt road marked Gata. After rounding the base of the mountain almost at water level, the road spirals up to vertiginous heights. On an awe-inspiring site overlooking the gorge stands Meštrović's statue of Mila Gojsalič, a peasant girl who died heroically during the Turkish raids of the mid-17th century. At night, Mila slipped into the Turkish pasha's tent and set fire to the powder magazine, blowing up the pasha and herself as well. Rather than be taken alive, the Turkish soldiers flung themselves over the cliff into the ravine.

Entering a mountain-ringed plateau, the road leads to the village of GATA, former capital of the self-governing communes of Poljica. Independent from the 11th century until Napoleon's Marshal Marmont

SOUTH OF SPLIT

sent in his troops, the people of Poljice elected their own princes and drew up a code of laws, which, according to scholars, may have given Sir Thomas More a few ideas for his *Utopia*.

South of Omiš, the road hugs the mountainside. Below, an occasional group of houses clings precariously to the steep slopes. Towards the sea, you have a continuous view of Brač island. Now and again you'll spot a small jetty forming a breakwater for fishermen's boats or the cabin cruiser of a tourist. A surprise in store for the springtime traveller is iris growing wild in wayside crevices.

About 20 kilometres from Omiš, a newly paved road branches over a mountain pass to the waterfalls and power plant at Zadvarje. Throughout this region, surface and underground waters have gouged canyons, caves and deep depressions out of the limestone rock. Near IMOTSKI are the Red and Blue Lakes. They were probably formed when the roofs of vast caverns collapsed, leaving deep abysses filled with water and rocky walls plunging down 500 feet. Native to the region is the fine white wine of Kujundžuša. Its name derives from the Turkish word *kuyum*, meaning gold.

The MAKARSKA RIVIERA features wide, sweeping slopes of pines, sheltered and cut off from the rest of the world by a towering wall of bald, grey mountains. In their shadow nestle a dozen seaside villages, quiet and sleepy until the

*Meštrović statue of local heroine overlooks awesome Cetina gorge.*

tourists arrive for the summer season.

The pines along the long pebble beaches of BRELA are so thick they screen the hotels, summer homes and old stone houses of the early settlers from the mountains. Some of the houses lining the steps that serve as streets still have the old stone roofs, freshly cemented in case of a sudden high wind.

Behind the villages of BAŠKA VODA and PROMAJNA, the early morning sun picks up the crags and fissures of the rugged mountains, dispelling the haze that blurs the contours of Brač island. If you think you've discovered the ideal place for a holiday, you're only following a well-established trend: archaeological diggings show that the Romans were here 2,000 years ago.

The thriving resort town of MAKARSKA (37 km. from Omiš) follows the curve of a horseshoe bay and spills over into another bay, where dense pine woods border one of the area's most popular beaches. The older part of the town backs up the palm-lined waterfront. Pressing in behind are the Biokovo mountains: the highest peak is only 9,000 feet away from the pier.

Makarska's Roman rule came to an end in 548, when the Ostrogoths sacked the town. Never fortified, Makarska was occupied by the Turks from 1499 to 1646. The Venetians and Austrians followed. And as if man hadn't wreaked enough havoc, an earthquake shook the town in 1962.

From the quay, a flight of steps leads up to the old town square named after poet Andrija Kačić-Miošić, a Franciscan friar, whose statue stands in the centre. But the real attraction here is a **seashell collection** in the Franciscan monastery (on Srećko Borić Street) which will delight all. Glass showcases contain shells of every hue: from a delicate pink to a deep purple, a giant clam that weighs over 200 pounds, yellow mollusks from China and even an oyster with a real pearl inside.

The Adriatic Highway continues south, keeping well above the villages, each just as inviting as the last. The island offshore is Hvar. A tall white monument, the stylized wings of a seagull, marks tiny PODGORA, where the Partisan navy

*No need to go to town: fresh fruit is brought by floating greengrocer.*

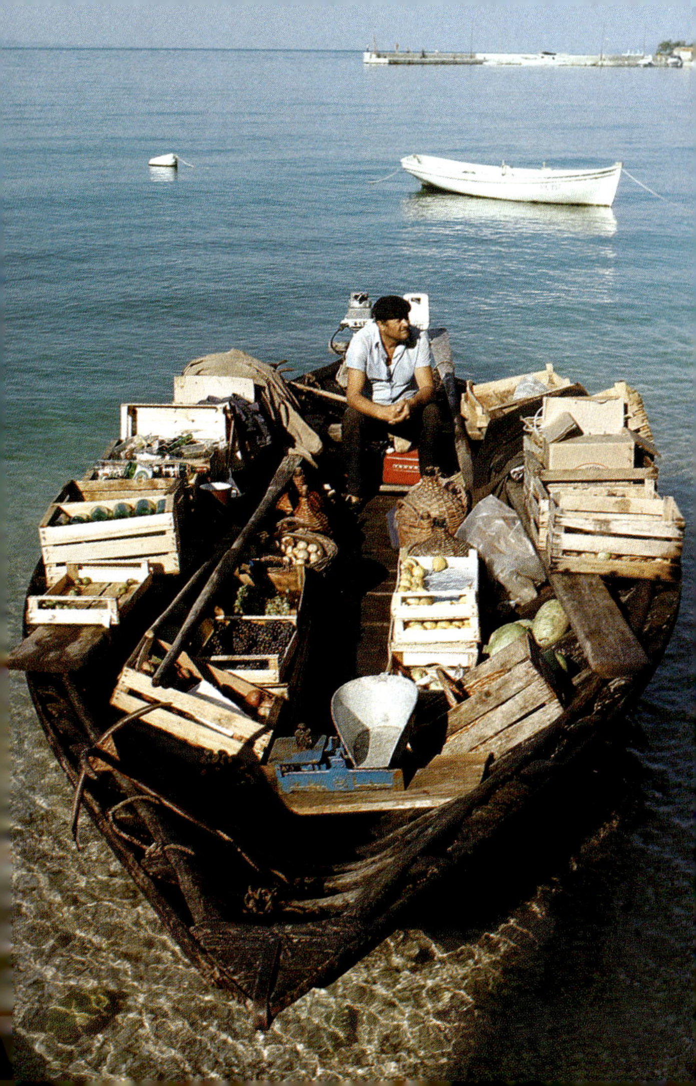

set up its first headquarters. New hotels perch on the rocky slopes, terraced with pink oleanders and scented jasmine.

The Makarska Riviera ends at GRADAC, its double row of houses facing the sea. Waves wash the white pebbles of the semi-circular beach, the pale-green translucent water deepening to turquoise.

## Mostar and Sarajevo

With mosques, minarets and oriental bazaars only a few hours away, you won't want to miss the historic city of Mostar. If you've a bit more time to spare you can travel further inland to Sarajevo, a big city with an exotic cast. You'll be impressed at how much this part of Yugoslavia just beyond the mountains differs from the coastal region.

On the 70-kilometre trip from KARDELJEVO on the coast to Mostar, an ideal spot to take a break is **Počitelj,** a walled town built by the Turks. Over a period of four centuries, they added fortifications, a mosque, a *medresa* (a Moslem theological school), public baths and a clock tower, which lost its bell in 1917; the Austrians melted it down to make bullets.

Carrying on toward Mostar, the road follows the river upstream, and the valley widens into a dusty plateau. Barely visible against the skyline are inaccessible fortresses. In the midst of this wasteland—an unlikely place for human habitation—you come upon the oriental city of **Mostar.** The minarets of its 24 mosques reach out above the rooftops. Fanning out from the town are vineyards, groves of fig trees and tobacco fields.

Dominating the scene is the torrential Neretva River, spanned by an ancient arched Turkish **bridge.** Built in 1566, this "bridge" *(most)* gave the town its name. As the story goes, an earlier attempt to span the river had failed. The sultan vowed to execute the architect if his next bridge didn't stand. The man who was responsible, Hajruddin, stalled as long as he could, but the day finally came to remove the supports. He had so little faith in his own project that he fled in fright and was later found digging his own grave. Hajruddin's pessimism couldn't have been less appropriate. The bridge still stands, a classic of engineering and art.

Not far from the bridge is the **mosque of Karadjoz Beg,** a local administrator of the mid-16th century. You may hear one of the five daily calls to prayer—no longer chanted by

*The Turkish bridge at Mostar enhances the town's Oriental aspect.*

the *muezzin* from the minaret balcony but played over a public-address system.

Here you'll occasionally see an old man in the timeless Moslem costume: a black-tassled red fez, a red cummerbund (in earlier times holding a pistol or dagger) and pointed leather slippers. And women wear those billowing Turkish pantaloons, but the veil is no longer worn.

On the narrow street leading to the old bridge each house is painted a different colour—a tradition of individualism carried on in the workshops. Follow the sound of hammering and you'll find an artisan crafting copper, silver or gold into delicate designs. See, too, the woollen carpets in bright geometrical patterns.

Leaving Mostar, the northbound road again follows the

Neretva canyon, now flanked by hills of naked rock. If you see a sign saying *hidroražanj*, it means lamb is roasting on a spit, turned by paddles in a mountain stream.

At **Sarajevo,** 130 kilometres from Mostar, a rapidly growing city of around half a million, the influences of East and West succeeded one another and now mingle. Site of the winter Olympics of 1984, it received a facelift and many new amenities —that's the modern side. The colourful old quarter runs along the embankment of the Miljacka River. One of the bridges is named after Gavrilo Princip, the Bosnian revolutionary who assassinated Austrian Archduke Franz Ferdinand on June 28, 1914, precipitating World War I. Two footprints set into the pavement mark the spot from which he fired. On the corner is a museum dedicated to the event and the conspirators, regarded locally as patriots.

Moving away from the river you enter **Baščaršija,** which was formerly the commercial centre of Sarajevo, a labyrinth of narrow streets and alleys lined with old, wooden-shuttered booths. Each street is named after the guild of artisans who operated there (Street of the Saddlemakers etc.). Fortunately, it's a pedestrians-only zone.

You'll know **Gazi Husref Beg's Mosque,** built in 1531, by its bluish-green oriental dome and slender minaret. The courtyard in front contains a fountain and two Turkish mausoleums *(turbe);* the stone turbans inside indicate the rank of the deceased. The mosque itself is carpeted with fabulous Persian rugs presented by Moslem dignitaries, past and present. Sarajevo's first school, a *medresa* built in 1537, and also a red-brick clock tower stand nearby.

Among the buildings recently restored are the covered market, Brusa Bezistan (1551), and an old Turkish caravanserai, or inn, called the Daire, with rooms opening onto a cobblestone courtyard. Mind your head going in.

If you climb up to the citadel, don't miss the lovely Turkish houses with their latticed windows (so women could peer out without being seen). Or if you prefer even greater heights, cross the river and take the cable-car up to Mount Trebević for another splendid view.

On your way out of Sarajevo, the Regional Museum *(Zemaljski muzej)* on Vojvode Putnika Street provides an overall survey of the changing

*Sarajevo's mosques and minarets recall centuries of Ottoman rule.*

cultures in this area. There are artefacts from the Stone, Bronze and Iron ages, Illyrian and Roman relics as well as regional ethnographic exhibits —costumes, musical instruments, pottery and household utensils.

# Islands off Split

### Brač Island
Pop. 14,000

Roman galleys stopping at the island of Brač loaded up with amphoras of wine and olive oil, rounds of cheese, blocks of white limestone. Though stone is still quarried and shipped to distant destinations, the island's other exports have dwindled. Economic development may have by-passed the island, but a delightful haven from the tensions of urban living remains.

In the early Middle Ages, the island's bounty caught the eye of a succession of neighbouring powers. Life by the sea grew so perilous that ancient settlements were abandoned for inland safety. When the Venetians gained control in the 15th century, fortified communities developed again along the coast.

Brač lies near enough to Split to be in the day-trip category. A steamer makes the journey daily to SUTIVAN in about 45 minutes. You can spend the day at the nearby beaches, catching the same steamer on its way back to the mainland. Or you can stay on board and get off at SUPETAR, the administrative centre of the island.

The Petrinović family's mausoleum in the town cemetery, the work of Yugoslav sculptor Toma Rosandić, merits a visit.

Stone for Diocletian's palace and the basilicas at Salona was quarried near SPLISKA. A relief of Hercules has protected stonecarvers here since the 3rd century. The largest quarries are located at PUČIŠĆA, a busy community that once boasted 13 castles. Few of them survive today. From POVJA, with the remains of a 5th-6th-century basilica and baptistery incorporated into the parish church, the steamer returns to Split.

On the opposite side of the island, BOL is a port of call for steamers en route to Hvar. Miles of pebble and sandy beaches, plus the only freshwater springs on the island, gave this attractive village a head start in the tourist trade. In peak season, visitors far outnumber the residents.

The most popular beach lies a few minutes to the west. A long spur of pebble and sand jutting out into the sea, it's constantly reshaped by waves and currents. Walking or hiking is an excellent way to get around. Take in the Dominican monastery; visit the village of MURVICA to see a medieval refuge known as the Dragons' Cave with fantastic monsters carved into the rock; or venture up Vidova Gora (2,560 feet), the highest peak on the Dalmatian islands.

Another stop for the Hvar steamer is MILNA. Its deep, protected harbour served briefly as a Russian naval base during the Napoleonic wars.

## Hvar Island
Pop. 11,000
Like Dubrovnik, the island of Hvar tends to be spoken of in superlatives. The "Madeira of the Adriatic" enjoys a yearly average of 2,715 hours of sunshine and a mean temperature

in January of 47°F, a few degrees higher than the rest of the coast. A patchwork of lavender, rosemary, olive and grapevine terraces covers the hills of the island, and palms, agaves, oleanders and bougainvillea proliferate in the gardens and parks.

This 43-mile sliver, the longest island in the Adriatic, has been inhabited since the Stone Age. The name Hvar derives from the Greek colony of Pharos founded at Stari Grad (4th century B.C.). A century later, the Illyrians returned only to be driven out by the Romans. Slav tribes began to settle here in the 7th century, and periods of Byzantine, Croatian and Croato-Hungarian rule followed. In 1278, pirate attacks prompted the prosperous islanders to seek the protection of Venice, which more or less maintained its sway for the next five centuries. Venetian rule was often disputed by popular revolts, bloodily suppressed: 20 rebels swung from the yardarms of the Venetian admiral's galley in 1514. During Napoleon's occupation of Dalmatia, the British and

*Sunny, sheltered Hvar served as winter quarters for Venetian navy.*

*Tourists dressed or undressed for the shore; also seen, traditional black worn with kerchief and apron.*

Russian navies seized key islands as bases. Hvar was held by the British from 1812 to 1813, then ceded to the Austrians.

The principal town—for many the most charming—bears the same name as the island. Founded as a Greek colony, **Hvar town** prospered under the Venetians: their Adriatic fleet wintered in its neat little harbour. Now you'll see motorboats moored here waiting to ferry bathers to the sandy beach at PALMIŽANA in the Pakleni islets just outside the harbour.

From the waterfront, a piazza *(Pjaca)* cuts deep into the town. To the left you'll see a 16th-century **loggia** with elegant arcades and a balustraded clock tower, both reconstructed several times. A street of steps climbs past medieval mansions and the shell of a Venetian-Gothic palace. When the Turks raided and burnt the town in 1571, the townspeople fled up these steps to the fortress.

The crenellated walls of the old town end at a fortress called Španjolo (1551), but what the Spanish had to do with it remains a mystery. You can dine and dance here under the stars in the evening, and the view is superb during the day. Higher still is Fort Napoleon, built, of course, by the French.

At the far end of the Pjaca, beyond a medieval well, is the **Cathedral of St. Stephen** *(Sveti Stjepan)*. Begun in 1560, it was completed much later. Note the Gothic choir stalls and a *Flagellation,* clearly inspired by Juraj Dalmatinac's panel in the cathedral of Split.

The long **Arsenal** runs along one side of the square. Its arched entrance on the waterfront was large enough to admit galleys. In 1612, the addition of a second storey turned it into a theatre, just 13 years after Shakespeare's Globe was built in London. The delightfully Baroque interior dates from 1800, when the theatre was renovated by a group of public-spirited citizens. Those who contributed were given boxes in the tiny auditorium.

Along the quay, past the Arsenal, is the lovely campanile of the 15th-century **Franciscan monastery.** The church possesses a number of 16th-century paintings by Italian and local masters. An outstanding *Last Supper,* attributed to Matteo Ingoli, can be seen in the refectory, now a museum.

Following the shore in the opposite direction brings you to the public beach and several hotel complexes. This is a favourite evening stroll. A string of lights weaves along the waterfront and spotlights focus on the fortress above.

In the busy piazza young artists, seemingly oblivious to the crowd of admirers and critics, sketch 20-minute portraits. Just by the souvenir stalls you may want to sniff the tiny bottles of lavender oil which the peasant women set out for sale on kitchen tables.

The scent of lavender, sometimes quite overpowering, pervades the island. When you visit other parts of Hvar, you'll see the terraced slopes covered with blue tufts of it, drying in the sun.

The road to STARI GRAD is part of the 300 kilometres of roadway built by the French during their brief stay in Dalmatia. Just off the waterfront at Stari Grad is the **summer villa** *(Tvrdalj)* of Croatian poet Petar Hektorović. This 16th-century gem has a delightful fish pond, enclosed by an arcaded promenade. The Dominican monastery nearby boasts a Tintoretto.

Attractive JELSA circles the head of a deep bay. Its freshwater spring supplies the whole island with water. The quiet village of VRBOSKA lies hidden inside a curving inlet, but to be on the safe side its founders built their church *(Sveta Marija)* in the shape of a huge fort, complete with crenellations and two circular bastions. The neighbouring church of St. Lawrence *(Sveti Lovrinac)* possesses a painting by Paolo Veronese.

## Vis Island
Pop. 4,000

Set far out in the Adriatic, the island of Vis is edged with steep limestone cliffs. Greeks sent by Dionysius the Elder, ruler of Syracuse, settled here in the 4th century B.C., planting the first grapevines in the region.

Note that at present foreign tourists are not allowed to visit Vis as the island is an important naval base. Apply to the military authorities first.

The strategic position of Vis gave the islanders front-row

*Two beauties caught this morning; above: music helps the work along.*

## Korčula Island
Pop. 18,000

Less than a mile from the mainland lies the wooded island of Korčula, about the size of Martha's Vineyard in Massachusetts or the Isle of Wight.

Famous for its wine and mild climate, Korčula is especially proud of its principal city of stone construction, an inspiration of medieval town planning. The streets of the cramped island follow a herringbone layout ingeniously arranged to baffle the wind. Religious and administrative buildings in Gothic and Renaissance style give the squares and lanes a serene grace.

seats for two historic naval battles: in 1811, when the British trounced the French, and in 1866 when Austrian forces defeated Italy. During World War II, Tito and his general staff set up their headquarters on the island.

Cruises go to the nearby island of Biševo to see the **Blue Grotto** (*Modra Špilja*). Small boats can slip in through the 5-foot clearance on calm days. Sunbeams penetrating an underwater fissure light the vast cavern with an iridescent blue.

Korčula's history just might extend as far back as the 12th century B.C., when, legend says, it was settled by the Trojans. In any case, Greek colonists lived there as early as the 4th century B.C.; it was then that the island's first coins were minted. About 33 B.C. Korčula was brutally Romanized by Octavian Augustus, the emperor who rejected the advances of Cleopatra. In the 9th century A.D.—after about three centuries of Byzantine rule—the island was settled by Croats from the Dalmatian mainland. The Venetians conquered Korčula in the well-rounded year of 1,000 and held on—except for some tumultuous intervals—for nearly eight centuries.

At the beginning of the 19th century the island bowed to a succession of heavyweight rulers: Austria, Britain, France and Russia. The British contributed the brooding Fort Wellington (1815) that sits on the hill overlooking the old town.

During World War II, the people of Korčula suffered heavy casualties and considerable damage to their historic buildings. But enough has been preserved to make **Korčula town** one of the Adriatic's most picturesque ports of call.

The town's geographical bull's-eye and leading architectural achievement is **St. Mark's Cathedral** *(Sveti Marko),* begun at the outset of the 15th century. During 150 years of construction the style changed from Gothic to Renaissance. Korčula's stonemasons enjoyed widespread fame through the centuries; this church with its ornate portal, eccentric gables and rosette window shows why. The interior reveals unusual furnishings and art works of historic interest, including two Tintoretto paintings.

The cathedral is the site of the town's favourite legend. It was from the campanile that 16th-century bell-ringers caught sight of an approaching fleet of Turkish galleys. In their distress, they overestimated the number of ships, but the danger was still very real. The able-bodied had already left Korčula. Only old men, women and children remained. Nonetheless, urged on by their archdeacon, the motley band manned the cannon, firing volley after volley at the galleys below. A storm blew up that gave the defenders a brief respite. But soon the enemy was back. Everybody rushed to the walls, marching single file round and round. The ruse

*Legend and history mingle in the old fortified city of Korčula.*

worked: believing the town to be defended, the Turks sailed away.

Next to the cathedral on the main square, the 14th-century **Abbot's Palace** has become a small museum *(Opatijska riznica)*. The exhibits range from embroidered church vestments to Renaissance paintings. A museum devoted to local history and culture occupies the Gabrielis Palace, a 16th-century mansion across the narrow square.

The **Guildhall** connected to All Saints' Church *(Svi Sveti)* possesses a rich collection of religious art, including some Cretan icons brought back by

Korčula seamen. The oldest church in Korčula is St. Peter's *(Sveti Petar)*, started in the 10th century. Nearby, a tall, narrow building—half residence, half museum—is billed as the birthplace of Marco Polo. Although the 14th-century explorer probably never set foot in the house, tradition does maintain that he came from Korčula. In any case, the view from the watchtower of "Marco Polo's house" eases the sting of the admission fee.

Near the elaborately carved main city gate, the town hall *(Vijećnica)* evokes memories of Venetian pomp with its stately Renaissance loggias. Also worth seeing are the surviving municipal fortifications, part of a wall that fully enclosed the city until the mid-19th century.

Altogether, the old city contains fewer than 300 buildings, by no means all habitable. Many dilapidated houses have been abandoned since the great plague of the 16th century.

Several times each season, local talent presents a distinctive folklore extravaganza. The *moreška* is an ancient sword dance clashing in symbolism of good versus evil, Korčula versus the invaders. The costumes, skill and enthusiasm of the dancers, as well as the potential danger of the swordplay, make it an exciting spectacle (see p. 74).

In the channel between Korčula and the mainland lie 20 small islands. The nearest, BADIJA, has been turned into a sports centre. On the others, you may see Mediterranean seals sunning themselves. Tourists can enjoy good fishing and swimming from the rocks.

### Island Menageries

One of Korčula's minor claims to fame is the existence of an unexpected variety of fauna. It's the only place in the Adriatic where wild jackals dwell. Fortunately, Korčula's jackals keep clear of tourist areas.

The neighbouring island of Mljet harbours a different zoological novelty: a large colony of mongooses. They're descended from a pair imported from India around the turn of the century expressly to eliminate a snake problem.

Now there's a mongoose problem.

## What to Do

### Folklore

Practically every town even faintly resembling a tourist resort receives the visit of folk-dancers. Travelling around on the coastal steamers, the troupes are mostly amateur, but standards run high. They're young and very enthusiastic.

These programmes offer a selection of songs and dances from various parts of the country. Circle dances *(kolo)* form the basis; the music, tempo and footwork vary. In the *lindjo* from the Dubrovnik area, someone calls out the steps with humourous asides, like in American square dancing. A sword dance from Rugovo often highlights the programme: excitement builds up as a turbaned drummer leads the dancers through their paces, never missing a beat even when flat on his back.

Dangerous dancing is also featured on Korčula, where the islanders perform the *moreška* sword dance, derived from an ancient morality play.

The main folkloric event of the area is definitely the *alka* tournament at Sinj. Though some of the participants may have just hopped off a plane, they all don ancient uniforms, cherished for generations, then pick up lances, swords, guns, shields and maces from the local museum. Squires and shield-bearers head the procession, leading a horse decked out in the original armour of the Turkish pasha's horse. The competing riders follow, last year's winner in front. Trumpets announce the beginning of the contest which involves spearing a suspended ring with a lance while riding at a full gallop.

The colourful folk costumes of Dalmatia are rarely seen outside of these spectacles. Country fairs, especially those geared to the tourist trade, are the exception. You can find the ancient costumes in the ethnographic museum of Split or Zadar. Note the contrast between the heavy, richly embroidered dress of the mountain folk and the flowing, lace-edged garments of the maritime region.

## Festivals

Though not as ambitious as the festival of Dubrovnik, Split's summer gala (July 15–August 15) takes place in a splendid setting. In the underground halls of the palace, the cloister of the Franciscan monastery or Diocletian's peristyle you can enjoy opera, theatre, ballet or concerts from Bach and Bizet to the Beatles. A pop-song festival is held in the colonnades facing the sea on July 3–5.

Elsewhere, look for notices of local festivities. Some regularly scheduled events include:

**Benkovac,** 10th of each month, a country fair for souvenir hunters and camera fans.

**Korčula,** from Easter to October, Thursday performances of the *moreška* sword dance (see p. 72).

Another warlike dance called the *kumpanija* is performed in the village of **Blato,** April 23. Drums and bagpipes accompany intricate swordplay, climaxed by the pirate captain losing his head.

**Omiš,** July, festival of Dalmatian singing groups, almost exclusively male. Each town sends their best to compete.

**Šibenik,** middle of August, summer drama and music festival in ancient settings.

**Sinj,** mid-August, a jousting tournament in full costume commemorating victory over the Turks (see p. 28).

**Split,** May, annual sailing regatta to Kaštel Stari.

**Trogir,** July 9–August 15, concerts of classical music.

**Vodice,** July 27, Fishermen's

Night. August: donkey races.

**Vrlika,** early August, a country fair known as the *dernek* to which peasants in Sunday costumes bring hand-crafted items.

**Zadar,** July, classical music in St. Donatus'.

## Nightlife

Up and down the Coast, excitement turns up in unexpected places. A fishing village may be hiding a discotheque as raucous as one could desire. A luxury hotel apparently inhabited only by prim museum-lovers may run a lively nightclub — floor show, dancing and all. Some of the bigger hotels have gambling casinos to round out the glamour. Roulette, chemin de fer, blackjack, craps and slot machines compete for your investment.

Travel agencies operate night cruises aboard floating dance palaces plying the Adriatic, with calls at a fishermen's village for more dancing and drinking.

*And after sundown, a 20th-century spectacle in a medieval setting.*

### Films

Even the small towns have cinemas. In most places the films are shown outdoors on summer nights; the natural air-conditioning, unlike indoor ventilation, always works. Most of the films are foreign. They're shown with the original soundtrack, be it English, French, Italian or Japanese. Subtitles translate into Serbo-Croatian.

Programmes are not continuous; each showing is a separate sitting. In small towns there are intermissions for changing reels.

## Museums and Galleries

In a region where whole towns are museum pieces, where the local supermarket may be housed in a Gothic mansion, where construction gangs are constantly unearthing Roman mosaics and fragments of ancient sculpture, one might expect museums crammed with precious *objets d'art*. Collecting, however, is a pastime to be indulged in during periods of peace, and history hasn't given many of these to Dalmatia. Nonetheless, you'll find some small museums where you can spend a pleasant half-hour or so.

*Take time out from the beach to see a bit of antiquity; waterside activities keep children busy all day.*

### Split

**Archaeological Museum,** Zrinjsko-Frankopanska 13: a collection of the finest pieces found in the Roman ruins at Salona (closed Monday).

**City Museum,** Papalićeva 5: a fine collection of 15th- to 18th-century weapons (closed Sunday).

**Ethnographic Museum,** Narodni trg: folk costumes, wood carvings, rustic implements.

**Ivan Meštrović Gallery,** Šetalište Moše Pijade 44: an impressive collection of works by Yugoslavia's best-known sculptor.

**Maritime Museum,** Trg braće Radića 7: model ships and exhibits illustrating a great maritime heritage.

**Museum of Croatian Archaeological Monuments,** Ognjen Price: highlighting this collection are carved fragments from medieval Croatian churches.

**Outside Split**
**Makarska, Malacological Museum,** fascinating seashells in the Franciscan monastery.

**Šibenik, Town Museum:** archaeological and ethnographical collections, exhibits illustrating the work of sculptor Juraj Dalmatinac.

**Zadar, Archaeological Museum:** beautifully mounted exhibits show the successive cultures in this area.

**Zadar, Ethnographic Museum:** folk costumes, handicraft items.

# For Children

All but the smallest tykes ought to enjoy the folklore shows, considering the kaleidoscope of costumes, rhythms and tunes.

Most children are very happy with seaside activities —swimming, collecting seashells and intriguing stones and constructing sandcastles. The larger hotels have their own playgrounds and children's paddling pools, table tennis or minigolf.

Boat rides provide an adventurous change of pace—either the local ferries or half-day cruises.

In Split, three attractions will appeal to children: the model ships in the Maritime Museum, the tiny aquarium on Marjan point—with its fascinating array of starfish, sea horses and other Adriatic specimens—and Marjan hill itself. The climb to the top is very gradual.

## Shopping

Buying trinkets can be one of the memorable features of a foreign holiday. As elsewhere, the Adriatic coast sells a few white elephants among the bargains. One tourist's prize catch is another's dust-catcher.

As for haggling over prices, this is a rare pursuit in Yugoslavia these days. It's almost entirely confined to outdoor markets where craftsmen sell their own work. All the major shops and most of the minor ones belong to unions with fixed prices marked on the goods. It would be futile to haggle in any of these shops and quite possibly offensive. But street pedlars and the owners of small handicraft shops may accept your challenge to negotiate the price.

Even if you've no interest in buying souvenirs, you'll enjoy browsing through the shops for their cross-section of regional crafts. In the non-tourist shops you can see how and what the Yugoslavs buy. Check on local fashions and prices. The food shops and supermarkets, too, are a short-cut survey of the standard of living—and its cost. You'll be surprised at the list of countries which export food, drink and household wares to Yugoslavia.

Shopping hours follow the typical Mediterranean pattern —early morning to early evening with a long break during the heat of the afternoon. Typically, shops stay open from about 8 a.m. to noon, closing for lunch and siesta and reopening at leisure from 5 to 8 p.m. However, a certain number of shops—mostly supermarkets—remain open all day without a break. These anti-siesta establishments are marked *non-stop*.

Split is the undisputed commercial centre of the region, with many handicraft and speciality shops in the heart of the

*How about a one-string fiddle?*

old town. However, in smaller resorts as well as the more obscure villages, you may find shops selling items unheard of elsewhere. If you've the time to spare, compare prices city-to-city and shop-to-shop.

Here are some items to look for. Knowledgeable travellers consider them either relatively cheap in Yugoslavia or unique —and sometimes both.

*Carpets.* Like many handiworks on sale along the coast, these originate in less sophisticated inland areas; original hand-loomed patterns.

*Copper ware,* including Turkish-style coffee grinders, pots and cups, exotic and inexpensive.

*Crystal.* Imaginative and relatively inexpensive, worth keeping an eye out for special pieces.

*Dolls.* Collectors can stock up on the national costumes of all the republics of Yugoslavia.

*Embroidery* ranges from handkerchiefs to lavishly decorated skirts and blouses.

*Footwear,* perhaps made before your eyes, sometimes in the bargain category.

*Gramophone records* are a bargain—folk-music, the classics or a Balkan version of a pop song.

*Lace,* like embroidery, is a

traditional skill in parts of Yugoslavia.

*Leather goods* —luggage, wallets, handbags—need a close look and comparative pricing.

*Postage stamps* make cheap, thoughtful gifts for collectors on your list.

*Posters and prints.* Another money-saving idea; look for cheap but good reproductions of charming contemporary Yugoslavian art.

*Pottery.* For instance, hand-painted plates in bright colours and one-of-a-kind designs.

*Spirits.* Very inexpensive, often impressively packaged gifts. Consider *maraskino* (morello-cherry flavour) and *šljivovica,* the plum brandy of renown.

*Wood carving.* Salad sets, statuettes, flutes, knick-nacks, mass-produced by hand.

*Woven fabrics.* Tablecloths, dress material, shoulder bags, in typical Yugoslavian patterns.

*Gift jewelry ranges from wooden beads to delicate silver filigree.*

# Sports and Other Activities

For the tourist seeking vehement exercise or just a paddle in unpolluted water, the shores of the Adriatic fill the bill for healthful outdoor recreation. Whatever your sport, watch out for too much sun. If you're shivering from the after-effects of sunburn, you're certainly not going to enjoy your holiday. An hour's excess exposure on opening day is enough to spoil everything. Do nothing drastic until your skin has become accustomed to the powerful rays. Wear a hat at midday. You can buy suntan lotion on the spot.

**Swimming** is the most basic way of enjoying the placid sea along the Dalmatian coast. Rocky coves, pebble beaches, man-made embankments and brief stretches of sand alternate from Zadar to the Makarska Riviera. Depending on the locale, the facilities may range from zero, or perhaps an elementary shower, to the parasols and pampering bar service on the beaches of luxury hotels.

**Snorkelling** gives the swimmer an undistorted, uninterrupted view of the undersea world. Sporting-goods shops in the towns sell masks, breathing tubes and flippers. Because of the exceptional transparency of the Adriatic and the proliferation of fish, these are splendid waters for the undersea fan.

**Scuba diving** is very tightly controlled. You need a permit from the local authorities in charge of internal affairs (address available from Tourist Office). Underwater fishing with diving equipment is forbidden. There are zones in which undersea activity is prohibited, such as the area of ports and military installations. Other areas out of bounds are the waters around Dugi Otok (northern part), Žirje and Kakan, the coastal waters from Šibenik to Trogir including the nearest islands, the channel between Pelješac and Korčula and around Vis Island.

**Boating.** If you're visiting Yugoslavia aboard your own yacht, you must apply for a sailing permit at your first port of call. Service facilities may be found in ports big and small. If you'd like to hire a yacht, this, too, can be arranged. A professional crew is optional. At certain beaches you can hire small sailing-boats. Rowing-boats and small motor-boats are also available on an hourly basis.

**Water-ski** instruction and equipment are provided at a dozen different beaches between Zadar and the Makarska Riviera.

A final seaside sport, **fishing**; the number of regulations seems to equal the number of species waiting to take your hook. For the latest instructions, check with the local authorities when you reach your resort. Equipment may be bought in sporting-goods shops in the towns. Incidentally, after you've gone through any formalities, you may find your daily catch is restricted to 5 kilograms (11 pounds). Hardly a morning's work, to hear some anglers tell it.

**Mountain-climbing** begins near the coast in the Dinaric Alps which dominate Dalmatia. Don't underestimate the mid-day sun at high altitudes.

**Hunting** expeditions to the interior for big game (bear, wild boar) can be arranged through Yugoslav travel agencies. But closer to the coast there's good duck hunting: near Lake Vrana (south of Zadar),

*For sports—fishing, water-skiing and a local version of ten-pins.*

at Hutovo Blato (just off the road for Mostar).

**Winter sports.** There's good skiing in the mountains around Sarajevo, site of the 1984 Winter Olympics. Downhill sites include Trevević, Bjelašnica and especially Jahorina. Cross-country enthusiasts should head for Igman.

## Spectator Sports

**Football.** Soccer is a serious pursuit in Yugoslavia and Hajduk Split is one of the country's leading teams, but the principal matches are held outside the tourist season. You may stumble onto less formal warm-ups locally.

**Water-polo.** Each Adriatic village seems to field a team ready to drown for local honour. An exciting game to watch when spirits reach flood tide.

## Other Pursuits

**Bowling** alleys have been opened in half a dozen major tourist hotels along the southern coast.

**Table-tennis** is very widely available.

**Chess** is more of a major national sport than in most Western countries. If you can play, it's a quick way to meet the Yugoslavs and get to know them.

# Flora and Fauna

The parched mountain slopes parallelling the Adriatic in Central Dalmatia support only the hardiest of vegetation. Sturdy pines and brush climb the lower reaches. Where the shallow soil has been terraced, groves of gnarled olive trees adjoin vineyards and an occasional fig tree. A group of cypresses, by tradition, marks a cemetery. In the towns, gardeners pamper oleanders, canna, jasmine and bougainvillea.

While wild hare, fox and wolves may be occasionally spotted in the hills, hikers interested in the more exotic fauna may quite easily discover bats. They're found in coastal caves and along the most isolated parts of the shore. Mediterranean seal also survive.

Bird-watchers may not be impressed by the cheerful resident sparrows and finches, but many transient birds are worthy of a second look: warblers, robins and thrushes are present in intriguing categories. Ducks, geese and heron inhabit the valleys.

The Adriatic Sea is home to hundreds of species—enchanting or gruesome, delicious or dangerous. Fishermen will often find eel, perch, bass and mullet. The open sea is rich in sardine, mackerel and tunny (tuna). Local menus confirm the proximity of squid, mussels and lobster.

Cautious swimmers will be relieved to learn that, while sharks do appear in the Adriatic, the blue or man-eating monsters are exceedingly rare.

*In early spring, a profusion of wild flowers dot the rocky slopes.*

# Wining and Dining

Good food stands high on the Yugoslavs' list of priorities, so whether you eat to live or live to eat, you can set about holiday wining and dining with confidence and pleasurable anticipation.

Seafood and pasta have been the mainstay of Adriatic cuisine for generations. Unfortunately, the sea is becoming less bountiful and, except in out-of-the-way corners, peak-season demand for freshly netted fish far exceeds the available supply. But don't worry. Diversity of culture produces diversity of cookery, and the specialities of other regions are well established up and down the coast. Just follow your nose, and you'll soon find a hooded charcoal grill with sizzling shishkebabs, spitted lamb or sucking pig. And to wash these delicacies down, a wide assortment of wines, many first-class and generally inexpensive.

But trying some of these exotic and tasty specialities often means venturing beyond

*A place to enjoy ambiance—plus a selection of local specialities.*

*Dalmatian smoked ham is superb!*

the hotel dining-room with its multilingual menus and "international" cuisine. Where to go? We make no recommendations, award no stars, whisper no tips. Last year's discovery may turn into this season's disappointment. Even at best, there's no accounting for taste. But we'll tell you what you ought to know before you decide where to dine and what to look for once you're glancing at the bill of fare.

Remember that the fanciest décor doesn't necessarily guarantee the best food. A modest, privately owned *gostiona* can often outdo the plushest establishment when it comes to local specialities. First, a rundown of the various types of eating places:

*Bife:* this is the way the Yugoslavs write *buffet*—a snack bar serving all kinds of drinks, sandwiches, cold cuts and sometimes hot meals.

*Ekspres restoran:* a bit short on atmosphere as a rule—a rough-and-ready, self-service café; limited menu but good for your budget.

*Kafana:* a term covering everything from a coffee-and-cake shop in a large hotel to a full-scale restaurant; alcoholic drinks available in any case.

*Mlečni restoran:* a dairy shop which deals in light meals, pancakes, pastry, yoghurt, milk and even coffee.

*Gostiona:* a village inn or smaller restaurant, often privately owned; home-cooked, wholesome food, prepared and served by the proprietor and his family. Some have rooms to let.

*Restoran:* just about any restaurant from the humble to the elegant.

*Slastičarna:* ice-cream parlour plus cake-shop serving espresso coffee, fruit juices, dozens of flavours of ice-cream, as well as oriental pastries for the sweet-toothed.

*Konoba:* a wine cellar where you can enjoy local wine in gay ceramic jugs and a snack.

## Eating Habits

Breakfast *(doručak)* is not a big production in Yugoslavia. In tourist hotels ham-and-egg breakfasts may be obtained, but generally it's a matter of coffee or tea, rolls or bread, butter and jam with perhaps a soft-boiled egg or piece of cheese on the side. Breakfast coffee *(bela kafa*—white coffee) is generally made with a coffee substitute. If you prefer, you can always bring a jar of instant coffee to the breakfast table and ask for hot water *(topla voda)* or hot milk *(toplo mleko)*. Most seaside hotels are accustomed to this practice; some even supply the instant coffee. If you sit at the same place for all meals, you can probably leave the jar on the table (the same applies to unfinished bottles of wine or other drinks). And tea drinkers who find the brew too weak for their taste, can bring along some extra tea bags and pop one in to strengthen the mixture, then ask for cold milk *(hladno mleko)*.

In mid-morning, you may come upon a café where the locals drop in for a second breakfast *(marenda)*, often in the form of a goulash or fish stew *(brodet)*. This naturally leads to a glass of wine, and that's the end of your sightseeing. On the other hand, "When in Rome..."

The main meal of the day is lunch *(ručak)* though a hefty dinner *(večera)* also figures in the plan. A principal difference between the two meals is that soup tends to be replaced by a cold first course in the evening.

Meal times depend on the level of sophistication of the clientele. In fishing villages, for instance, dinner is over early. Elsewhere it could run till 10 or 11 p.m. In hotels, breakfast is served from about 7 to 9 a.m., lunch from noon to 2 p.m. and dinner from 7 to 9.

Most restaurants add a service charge to bills. Leaving a tip is customary: 5-10 per cent would be normal. Don't feel shy about checking a bill if it's more than you expected. By law, prices must be listed on the menu or, in smaller restaurants, posted.

Some restaurants offer fixed-price menus *(turistički meni)*, usually three courses without wine and a limited choice.

A menu is a *jelovnik,* and here are some of the treats to look for:*

### Appetizers

*Istarski* or *Dalmatinski pršut:* smoked ham, a distinctive delicacy of the coast, justly famous for its subtle flavour.

*Gavrilovićeva salama:* a tangy salami reminiscent of the best from Italy.

*Kajmak:* made with the skin of scalded milk, it has a unique flavour and cheesy texture.

### Soups

Categorized either as *juha,* a broth, or *čorba* (a thick soup), they come in many varieties and may be grouped together as *juha.*

### Fish and Shellfish

According to an old saying, the Adriatic can produce a different kind of fish for every day in the year. Only a fraction ever appear on the table. Mackerel and sardines, grilled or fried, are the most commonly served. For more distinguished fare, choose bass, dentex or bream, grilled slowly over coals. Pungent fish stews *(brodet),* often served with *palenta,* a purée of maize (cornmeal), are native to the region, recipes varying from village to village. Another way of preparing fish is *lešo* (poached).

Shellfish—lobster, or more often crab, oysters, shrimp, mussels—though delicious, are rather expensive. Boiled lobster, or crab, usually served cold with mayonnaise, is a delicacy. Mussels, steamed open or tossed in a *rizoto* (rice dish), are another speciality.

### Meat Dishes

Charcoal-grilled meat *(roštilj)* is perhaps the most ubiquitous item on Yugoslav menus. The best is usually to be found in restaurants, large or small, with an outdoor barbecue. Most popular as a supper dish, *roštilj* comes in all shapes and sizes, invariably served with chopped raw onion and often accompanied by a salad. Among them:

*Ćevapčići:* small sausage-shaped meat rolls (beef or beef-pork mixture); ten is the usual portion.

---

* For a comprehensive glossary of Serbo-Croatian wining and dining, ask your bookshop for the Berlitz EUROPEAN MENU READER.

*A delicious—and expensive—holiday treat: fresh-caught lobster.*

*Pljeskavica:* a large hamburger steak. If you don't like spicy food, say *"ne ljuto"* ("not hot") when ordering.

*Ražnjići:* skewered chunks of pork *(svinjski)* or veal *(teleći)*; two skewers, the usual portion.

*Ćulbastija:* grilled pork.

Order meat grilled over the coals *(na žaru)*, or go all the way and order one of the huge mixed grills *(mešano meso)*. Under the heading *Gotova jela* you'll find some tasty local specialities, mostly eaten at lunch time.

*Djuveč:* as if to prove that there's more to Yugoslavian cooking than kebabs, the Serbs invented this casserole dish of lamb or pork with rice, green pepper, eggplant, carrots, potatoes, cheese and whatever else captures the chef's imagination.

*Sarma:* an easy-to-pronounce, homey dish, this is cabbage leaves stuffed with minced meat and rice.

*Musaka:* layers of minced meat sauce alternating with potato, eggplant or courgettes (zucchini), baked.

*Punjene paprike:* green peppers stuffed with meat and rice in tomato sauce.

*Pastičada:* beef braised in wine served with noodles.

The more cautious diner can always order roast *(pečenje)*, specifying "hot" *(toplo)* or "cold" *(hladno)*.

### Fowl and Game

*Piletina* (chicken) and *ćuretina* (turkey) are commonly found on menus. But during hunting season you may want to try a more elusive bird such as *jarebica* (partridge) or *fazan* (pheasant).

### Salads and Vegetables

Salads most frequently accompany the main dish in both simple and elegant restaurants. A favourite is *srpska salata* (Serbian salad), a refreshing plate of tomatoes and onion. Another is *pečene paprike*, fried green pepper sprinkled with oil. Boiled vegetables also appear on the menus in season.

### Cheese
Two authentic local cheeses are *Paški sir*, a hard, strong cheese from the island of Pag, and *Kačkavalj*, a medium-hard cheese of variable quality.

*The island of Pag produces strong, hard cheese out of sheep's milk.*

Good locally produced versions of popular European cheeses are widely available. For Yugoslavs, by the way, cheese is a starter rather than a final course, but no one will mind if you reverse the order.

### Desserts
If you're not weight-watching, round off your meal with pancakes *(palačinke)* with ground nuts, jam or chocolate sauce. Sweet-lovers rave about the *baklava,* flaky pastry steeped in syrup, and other Turkish delights. Cream cakes and pastries of the Viennese type are often better in cake shops than in restaurants. The same applies to ice-cream.

### Wines and Beer
Since the best Yugoslav wines are rarely found outside the country, you've some delightful surprises in store. Not least is the price—very reasonable by Western standards, especially when bought in a shop or wine cellar.

Table wine *(stolno vino)* sold by the carafe is usually the local vintage, but none the worse for that. You can order as little as *tri deci* (three-tenths of a litre) to experiment. *Bjelo* (or *bijelo*) is white, *ružica,* rosé and *crno* (literally, black) means red wine. The locals often dilute it in the glass with soda or plain water.

Supermarkets in bigger resorts sell a bewildering variety of wines from all over Yugoslavia. Here are some of the outstanding ones you might meet:

*Dingač:* a full-bodied red from the Pelješac peninsula south of Split.

*Grk:* no vowels but plenty of punch in this strong white from the island of Korčula.

*Kutjevo:* varied wines of high standard from northern Croatia.

*Prošek:* a tawny-coloured dessert wine made along the coast from dried fermented grapes.

*Vugava:* a heady golden wine produced on the islands of Vis and Brač.

*Žilavka:* a delicate white wine from Herzegovina.

Among the best-known Istrian wines are the reds, *Teran* (more powerful) and *Refoško* (lighter), and the whites, *Malvazija* (may be sweet or dry) and *Pinot*. The Kvarner Islands have a number of good wines as well.

Slovenia produces some fine white wines *(Ljutomer Riesling, Jeruzalem, Ritoznojčan)*, not to mention the abundant output of Serbia and Macedonia.

If your thirst requires beer *(pivo)*, Yugoslavian lagers are sold in pint bottles. Imported brands, which are more expensive, come in smaller bottles.

**Other Beverages**
Bottled fruit juice *(voćni sok)* makes a refreshing drink—apricot, blueberry, peach, raspberry, strawberry, sour (morello) cherry, all trucked in from orchard country. Other soft drinks are also available, including several brand names, bottled locally. Prices for soft drinks, or any other kind of liquid refreshment, vary tremendously according to the ambiance, but they are posted in full view or listed on the menu. Tea drinkers are likely to be disappointed.

Although the Yugoslavs are great coffee drinkers, at virtually any hour of the day or night, the coffee served in public places rarely compares favourably with what is drunk in the homes. Good espresso coffee is dispensed practically everywhere along the coast. If the normal half cup isn't enough, ask for a double portion *(dupli)*. Some cafés also serve *cappuccino* and *eis kafe* (iced coffee with a scoop of ice-cream and whipped cream). Turkish coffee, served in tiny, long-handled pots, is a newcomer to these parts and not available everywhere. Its quality varies.

**Liquor**
Pre-dinner cocktails, a foreign invention, can be managed in many hotel bars. A Yugoslavian aperitif, milder than most, is *Istra Bitter*, a herb tonic. Imported brands of aperitifs, whiskies and other spirits are expensive.

*Rakija* is the generic term embracing all the brandies you're likely to find.

*Šljivovica,* plum brandy, is the most famous and popular Yugoslavian liquor.

*Lozovača* (grape brandy) and *kajsijevača* (apricot brandy) are alternative firewaters, according to your taste.

And don't forget *maraskino,* the liqueur made from maraschino, or morello, cherries.

Finally, *vinjak* is a local brandy reminiscent of a French cognac.

## To Help You Order...

Could we have a table? **Možemo li dobiti sto?**
The menu, please. **Molim Vas, jelovnik.**
The bill, please. **Molim Vas, račun.**
(I'd like some) ... please. **Molim Vas, ...**

| | | | |
|---|---|---|---|
| beer | **pivo** | napkin | **salvetu** |
| bread | **kruh** | potatoes | **krompir** |
| coffee | **kavu** | rice | **rižu** |
| cutlery | **pribor za jelo** | salad | **salatu** |
| dessert | **dezert** | sandwich | **sendvič** |
| fish | **ribu** | soup | **juhu** |
| fruit | **voće** | sugar | **šećer** |
| glass | **čašu** | tea | **čaj** |
| ice-cream | **sladoled** | water | **vodu** |
| meat | **meso** | wine | **vino** |
| milk | **mlijeko** | well-done | **dobro pečeno** |
| mineral water | **mineralnu vodu** | with ice | **sa ledom** |

## ... and Read the Menu

| | | | |
|---|---|---|---|
| **ananas** | pineapple | **fažol** | dried beans |
| **bakalar** | codfish | **file** | fillet |
| **barbun** | red mullet | **fileki** | tripe |
| **biftek** | beefsteak | **gljive** | mushrooms |
| **blitva** | Swiss chard | **govedina** | beef |
| **borovnice** | blueberries | **grašak** | peas |
| **brancin** | sea-bass | **grožđje** | grapes |
| **breskve** | peaches | **gulaš** | goulash |
| **bubrežnjak** | tenderloin | **hladno** | cold |
| **cipal** | grey mullet | **hobotnica** | octopus |
| **češnjak** | garlic | **hrenovka** | hot dog |
| **čokolada** | chocolate | **jabuka** | apple |
| **čorba** | thick soup | **jagnjetina** | lamb |
| **ćufte** | meatballs | **jagode** | strawberries |
| **ćulbastija** | grilled veal or pork | **jaja** | eggs |
| | | **jastog** | lobster |
| **dagnje** | mussels | **jetra** | liver |
| **dinja** | melon | **junetina** | baby beef |
| **divljač** | game | **kalamari** | squid |

| | | | |
|---|---|---|---|
| kamenice | oysters | paprika | green pepper |
| kavijar | caviar | pečenje | roast |
| keks | biscuits (cookies) | piletina | chicken |
| kiselo mleko | yoghurt | pljeskavica | hamburger steak |
| kobasice | sausages | | |
| kompot | stewed fruit | povrće | vegetables |
| kotlet | chop | prepržen kruh | toast |
| kovač | John Dory (fish) | prstaci | mussels |
| krastavac | cucumber | pršuta | smoked ham |
| krem | cream pudding | prženo | fried |
| krompir | potatoes | račići | shrimp |
| kruška | pear | ragu | stew |
| kuhano | boiled | rajčica | tomato |
| kupus | cabbage | rak | crab |
| lešo | boiled | riba | fish |
| lignji | squid | riža | rice |
| limun | lemon | salama | salami |
| list | sole | salata | salad |
| lubenica | watermelon | sardela | anchovy |
| luk | onion | sendvič | sandwich |
| mahune | string beans | sir | cheese |
| maline | raspberries | skampi | prawns |
| marelice | apricots | skuša | mackerel |
| maslac | butter | sladoled | ice-cream |
| masline | olives | smokve | figs |
| meso | meat | svinjetina | pork |
| mešano | mixed | školjke | shellfish |
| mladica | trout | špinat | spinach |
| mrkva | carrots | šunka | ham |
| mušule | mussels | teletina | veal |
| na gradele | | toplo | hot |
| na roštilju | grilled | torta | cake |
| na žaru | | trešnje | cherries |
| na ražanj | barbecued on a spit | tunina | tunny (tuna) |
| | | umak | sauce |
| nar | pomegranate | vešalica | grilled veal or pork |
| narandža | orange | | |
| odojak | sucking pig | višnje | sour cherries |
| odrezak | cutlet | vrgnji | mushrooms |
| orada | bream | vrhnje | whipped cream |
| oslić | hake | zelena salata | lettuce salad |
| ovčetina | mutton | zubatac | dentex (fish) |

# How to Get There

The central Adriatic coast is easily accessible by road, rail, sea or air. Your travel agent can help you find the right combination and give you the latest information on rates and regulations for air travel.

## BY AIR

**Scheduled Flights**

**From the British Isles:** There are a few direct flights to Split from London; otherwise, you may go by way of Zagreb. Tourists from other U.K. airports can make good connections in London or Zagreb.

**From North America:** There is regular direct service to Belgrade from Chicago and New York. Daily connecting flights may be booked from another two dozen American cities as well as four in Canada: Calgary, Montreal, Toronto and Vancouver. More than 40 cities in the U.S. have flights to Belgrade on specific days of the week (usually not Mondays and Thursdays). From Belgrade, there are frequent connecting services to Split.

**Charter Flights and Package Tours**

**From the British Isles:** The all-inclusive package tour—combining flight, hotel and board—remains a most popular way of visiting Split. Many travel agents recommend cancellation insurance, a modestly priced safeguard: you lose no money if illness or accident forces you to cancel your holiday.

**From North America:** Tours of Yugoslavia vary from three to 11 nights. The all-inclusive price covers hotel accommodation, airport transfers, all or most meals, sightseeing, English-speaking tour guide, plus hotel taxes and service charges. Yugoslavia can also be visited on tours of Eastern Europe and Russia.

## BY CAR

Yugoslavia is connected by good roads to neighbouring Italy, Austria, Hungary and Greece. You'll be able to drive on motorways (expressways) almost all the way. After crossing the border, you can get on the Adriatic Highway *(Jadranska magistrala)* which loops around Istria then follows the coast to Senj and beyond.

In July and August, with ferry space at a premium, be sure to book well in advance. Here's how you can go:

1. Via France: Dover–Boulogne/Calais/Dunkirk; Folkestone–Boulogne/Calais; Newhaven–Dieppe; Southampton–Cherbourg/Le Havre; Ramsgate–Dunkirk.

2. Via Belgium: Dover–Ostend/Zeebrugge; Folkestone–Ostend; Felixstowe/Hull–Zeebrugge.

3. Via Holland: Harwich–Hook van Holland; Hull–Rotterdam; Sheerness–Vlissingen.

4. For a slightly higher price than the ferry, you can cross by hovercraft from Dover to Calais (35 minutes) or to Boulogne (39–45 minutes). You can drive through Italy and then take a car-ferry to Yugoslavia, crossing at Ancona (for Zadar) or Pescara (for Split).

If you don't fancy the three- to five-day drive across Europe, put your car on a train (Brussels–Ljubljana or Paris–Munich–Rijeka) and then take to the wheel again in Ljubljana or Rijeka and sightsee refreshed. Both services operate only during the summer season, however. The car-sleeper motor-rail express, while expensive, saves on fuel, wear-and-tear and hotel bills.

## BY RAIL

Yugoslavia is connected by rail with all European countries. The trip from London to Split takes about a day and a half.

**Eurailpass:** Anyone except residents of Europe can travel on a flat-rate, unlimited mileage ticket valid anywhere in western Europe outside Yugoslavia and Great Britain. You must sign up before leaving home. **Inter-rail pass:** This fixed-rate pass for one month's unlimited second-class rail travel throughout most of Europe, including Yugoslavia, is available to anyone under 26. **Rail Europ Senior Card:** Women over 60 and men over 65 can purchase this card for unlimited travel, allowing a discount of 30 to 50%.

# When to Go

Central Dalmatia enjoys the mild climate of the Mediterranean, neither too hot in summer nor too cold in winter—and Split itself ranks as one of the sunniest places in Europe. Winter temperatures seldom drop below 41°F, and the nearby island of Hvar averages several degrees higher. Split's northern side is protected by Mount Mosor, and a sea breeze freshens even the sultriest days. Chilly and rainy spells are rare.

You can usually swim in the sea from spring to late autumn, and many hotels offer indoor pools with heated sea water.

|  |  | J | F | M | A | M | J | J | A | S | O | N | D |
|---|---|---|---|---|---|---|---|---|---|---|---|---|---|
| **Air temperatures** |  |  |  |  |  |  |  |  |  |  |  |  |  |
| Max. | F | 50 | 51 | 53 | 65 | 72 | 82 | 86 | 86 | 79 | 67 | 58 | 54 |
|  | C | 10 | 11 | 12 | 18 | 22 | 28 | 30 | 30 | 26 | 19 | 14 | 12 |
| Min. | F | 41 | 41 | 45 | 52 | 59 | 68 | 72 | 71 | 66 | 57 | 49 | 46 |
|  | C | 5 | 5 | 7 | 11 | 15 | 20 | 22 | 22 | 19 | 14 | 10 | 8 |
| **Sea temperatures** |  |  |  |  |  |  |  |  |  |  |  |  |  |
|  | F | 55 | 53 | 53 | 55 | 66 | 70 | 75 | 75 | 71 | 68 | 63 | 58 |
|  | C | 13 | 12 | 12 | 13 | 19 | 21 | 24 | 24 | 22 | 20 | 17 | 14 |

All figures shown are approximate monthly averages.

# BLUEPRINT for a Perfect Trip

## An A-Z Summary of Practical Information and Facts

> Listed after each main entry is its appropriate Serbo-Croatian translation, usually in the singular. You'll find this vocabulary useful when asking for assistance. Because of the linguistic variations you may encounter in different regions, an alternative translation is sometimes indicated in brackets []. If the first expression brings a blank look, try the second.

**A**  **ACCOMMODATION**—see **HOTELS**

**AIRPORT** *(aerodrom)*. The principal airport serving the central Dalmatian coast is at Kaštel Štafilić, 25 kilometres north of Split, just off the Adriatic Highway. Porters are generally available to carry your bags to the taxi rank or bus stop. Buses operate regularly between city and airport, but arriving tourists are normally met by airline or travel-agency coaches taking them straight to their hotel. The airport terminal includes a currency-exchange counter, car-rental and travel-agency offices, a duty-free shop and a snack-bar.

Check-in for international flights is 70 minutes before departure. If you're taking the airport bus, allow 80 minutes from Split.

There is an airport departure tax both for domestic and international flights.

Another airport at Zemunik, 12 kilometres east of Zadar, handles primarily domestic and charter flights.

| | |
|---|---|
| Porter! | **Nosač!** |
| Taxi! | **Taksi!** |
| Where's the bus for…? | **Gde je autobus za…?** |

**ALPHABET.** Two alphabets are used in Yugoslavia: the familiar Latin one and the Cyrillic, similar to Greek or Russian, used in Serbia, Montenegro, Bosnia and Macedonia. You're unlikely to see Cyrillic except on news-stands. Both alphabets are completely phonetic, so it's easy to read Serbo-Croatian once you know how each letter is pronounced. Most letters of the Latin alphabet are pronounced much as in English; the exceptions are explained in the table below:

| | | | | | |
|---|---|---|---|---|---|
| A | c*a*r | C | ba*ts* | J | *y*oke |
| E | g*e*t | Č | *ch*urch | LJ | fai*l*ure |
| I | l*ea*p | Ć | crun*ch*ier | NJ | o*n*ion |
| O | h*o*t | DŽ | *j*eep | Š | *sh*ip |
| U | b*oo*m | DJ | *s*oldier | Ž | plea*s*ure |

**BABYSITTERS** *(čuvanje dece)*. Except in luxury hotels, babysitting facilities aren't likely to be available on an organized basis. Especially in out-of-the-way spots, somebody's grandmother will probably be recruited; otherwise you can contact the student service *(studentski servis)* in Split, Sinskih žrtava 6 (tel. 41-854), which should be able to arrange for a babysitter to come to your hotel.

Can you get us a babysitter for tonight?   **Možete li nam naći nekog da čuva decu večeras?**

**BANKS and CURRENCY-EXCHANGE OFFICES** *(banka; menjačnica)*. Banks open early in summer—7 a.m. in many resorts—and close anywhere from 11.30 a.m. to 7 p.m.

When banks are closed or too far away, you can change money at identical rates in authorized currency-exchange offices including travel agencies and hotels. Though currency-exchange operations may close a few hours for lunch, they usually remain open until early evening.

Try to assess how much dinar cash you will need, because excess cash cannot be reconverted (this does not apply to dinar cheques; see CREDIT CARDS AND TRAVELLERS' CHEQUES), and only a small amount can be exported (see CUSTOMS CONTROLS).

I want to change some pounds/ dollars.   **Želim da promenim funte/ dolare.**

**BARBER'S**—see **HAIRDRESSER'S**

99

**B** **BICYCLES** *(bicikl)*. Bicycles can be hired by the hour in only a few resorts. Other two-wheeled vehicles can be purchased, but it's not possible to hire one for getting around on the coast.

**BOAT SERVICES** *(brodske veze)*. Passenger steamers, car ferries and fast hydrofoils operate regularly up and down the coast and from the mainland to the islands. During the peak summer months, the car ferries are particularly crowded, so you may have to leave your car on the mainland. Tickets can be purchased at the Jadrolinija office on the dock or even on board. It's better to book cabins for overnight trips well in advance. Refreshments are usually available on board.

Main services: Split–Vis–Komiža, Split–Vrboska (Hvar), Split–Sutivan (Brač), Split–Trogir–Drvenik, Šibenik–Zlarin–Žirje, Šibenik–Zlarin–Vodice, Zadar–Olib–Silba, Zadar–Mali Lošinj.

**Car Ferries** *(trajekt)*. Fares depend on the size of the car and the number of passengers; the driver goes free.

Main services: Split–Stari Grad (Hvar), Split–Vira (Hvar), Drvenik–Sućuraj (Hvar), Split–Supetar (Brač), Makarska–Sumartin (Brač), Orebić–Korčula, Zadar–Preko (Ugljan).

**BOY MEETS GIRL.** Attitudes towards life are relaxed along the Adriatic. The flirtation is comparable to anywhere else in Europe. As in most countries, however, beware that small towns are much more strict than cities and tourist zones. If you haven't made friends on the beach, try the *korzo*—the community promenade—at sunset. In every town, the main square or street is a meeting point for all the young people who stroll and chat and look the field over to plan the evening's activities.

**BUS SERVICES.** Railways being few and far between in this area, the regional bus transport is highly developed and usually comfortable. In most towns, there's a bus station where you can book in advance. As the timetables tend to be complicated, you're safer enquiring about schedules at your hotel or local tourist office. Sometimes an excursion is cheaper by regular bus than by an organized coach trip (see EXCURSIONS). Bus services between Split and nearby beaches are frequent.

Avoid city transport at crowded peak hours (7 a.m., 2 p.m., early evening). The number of passengers is limited only by the capacity of the vehicle and human stamina. Queuing up is a relatively new practice, not usually observed at bus stops. You get on most city buses at the back door and pay the conductor. Tickets bought at newsstands are cheaper.

| When's the next bus to...? | **Kad ide sledeći autobus za...?** |
| How much is the fare to...? | **Koliko košta do...?** |
| single (one way) | **u jednom pravcu** |
| return (roundtrip) | **povratnu kartu** |
| Will you tell me when to get off? | **Hoćete li mi, molim Vas, reći kad treba da sidjem.** |

**CAMPING** *(kampovanje)*. Few camping areas in Europe rival the Yugoslav Adriatic. In central Dalmatia alone, there are over 30 camps, often in wooded locations by the shore.

Rates depend on the setting and the variety of services offered. A local tourist tax is always added to the bill.

No special permit is required for camping but you have to use an authorized site. Just pulling up at the side of the road for the night is illegal.

A free list of camps throughout Yugoslavia is published in English each year by the Automobile Association of Yugoslavia (AMSJ). The list is available at tourist offices or direct from AMSJ (address: Obala Lazareta 3, Split).

| Is there a campsite near here? | **Da li ima kamp u blizini?** |
| May we camp here? | **Možemo li ovde kampovati?** |
| We've a tent/caravan (trailer). | **Imamo šator/prikolicu.** |
| What's the charge...? | **Koliko košta...?** |
| per person | **po osobi** |
| for a car | **za kola** |
| for a tent | **za šator** |
| for a caravan | **za prikolicu** |

**CAR-RENTAL** *(rent a kar)*. Half a dozen car-rental firms operate along this part of the coast, in Split, Šibenik, Zadar, Makarska, and at the two airports serving the area. Your hotel receptionist or travel agency representative will be able to organize things if you haven't reserved ahead.

There are innumerable variants in price depending upon the firm involved, the model of car, the length of time you use it and whether you plan to return it to the same place or elsewhere inside Yugoslavia or abroad. The most frequently rented cars are Volkswagen, Audis, Fiats and Renaults. You can rent a Mercedes 220, but it'll cost twice the price of a VW. Chauffeured cars may also be arranged.

You must pay a refundable deposit unless you hold an internationally recognized credit card. A local tax may or may not be included in the rate. Non-deductible collision insurance and accident insurance covering driver and passengers come extra.

You must, of course, hold a valid driving licence at least one to two years old, depending on the firm. The minimum age varies from 21 to 25.

Car-rental firms are generally open from 8 a.m. to 8 p.m. with an early-afternoon break.

Fuel and traffic fines are the customer's responsibility.

| | |
|---|---|
| I'd like to rent a car tomorrow. | **Hteo bih da rentiram kola sutra.** |
| for one day/a week | **za jedan dan/jednu nedelju** |
| Please include full insurance. | **Sa potpunim osiguranjem molim Vas.** |

**CHURCH SERVICES.** Mass in Latin or Serbo-Croatian is said daily in many towns of this predominantly Roman Catholic region. There is a Protestant church at Zagrebačka 4 in Split. Hotels or travel agencies occasionally plan services for non-Catholic church-goers.

There is a synagogue at Židovski prolaz 1 in Split.

| | |
|---|---|
| What time is mass? | **U koliko sati je misa?** |

**CIGARETTES, CIGARS, TOBACCO** (*cigarete, cigare, duvan*). Yugoslavian cigarettes come in a strong, black Turkish variety as well as in mild blends similar to British or American cigarettes. In addition to many local makes, certain American brands are manufactured in Yugoslavia under licence. In larger towns and resorts a few British brands may also be found. As in most countries, the local cigarettes cost only a fraction of the retail price of the imports.

Tobacco shops also sell imported (usually Cuban) cigars and Yugoslavian pipe tobacco, which is highly regarded by connoisseurs.

| | |
|---|---|
| A packet of cigarettes/matches. | **Kutiju cigareta/šibica.** |
| filter-tipped | **sa filterom** |
| without filter | **bez filtera** |
| light tobacco | **blagi duvan** |
| dark tobacco | **ljuti duvan** |

**CLOTHING** *(odevanje)*. With its Mediterranean climate, the central Adriatic coast demands lightweight clothing from June to September—the lighter the better. But on the fringes of the high season—before July and after August 30—you may well need a jacket or sweater for the evening. Although the rainy season comes in winter, you could need a raincoat at any time of year.

Formality in dress is confined to sophisticated night-clubs and casinos. Elsewhere it's a matter of pleasing yourself. That goes for beaches as well; no prudish anti-bikini sentiments here. However, it's reasonable to slip something over your bathing suit for the walk to and from the beach.

Obviously, when visiting churches modest dress is appropriate. And don't forget to wear your comfortable shoes when you go visiting museums or sightseeing.

**COMPLAINTS** *(žalba)*. Complaint procedures are far less formalized in Yugoslavia than they've become in some other countries.

**Hotels and restaurants.** See the manager if you're dissatisfied. If this leads nowhere, the local tourist office may suggest further steps.

**Bad merchandise.** The consumer-oriented society is too new in Yugoslavia to have devised elaborate safeguards. Your best bet here is to return to the shop which sold you the article and appeal to the manager's sense of fair play.

**Car repairs.** If your car has been badly repaired, or if you believe you've been overcharged, try to settle the problem before paying the bill. If this fails, a local travel office may be able to mediate or advise.

**Other services** (shoe repairs etc.). By law, prices should be posted, but to avoid misunderstanding, it's wise to ask the cost of all services in advance.

**CONSULATES** *(konzulat)*

**British Consulate:**\* Obala Maršala Tita 10/11, Split; tel. 41-464.
**Canadian Embassy:** Proteterskih brigada 69, Belgrade; tel. 434-524.
**U.S. Consulate:** Zrinjski trg 13, Zagreb; tel. 444-800.
**U.S. Embassy:** Kneza Miloša 46, Belgrade; tel. 645-621.

---

\* also for citizens of Eire and Commonwealth countries not separately represented.

**C** Where's the British/American/ Canadian Consulate?
It's very urgent.

**Gde je Britanski/Američki/ Kanadski konzulat?
Veoma je hitno.**

**CONVERSION TABLES.** For tire pressure, distance and fluid measures—see pp. 108-109. Yugoslavia uses the metric system.

**Temperature**

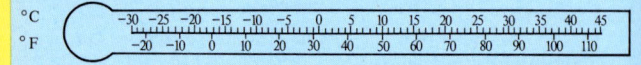

°C / °F scale from −30°C to 45°C / −20°F to 110°F

**Length**

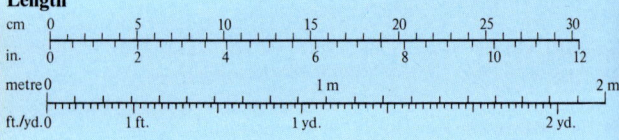

cm: 0 to 30
in.: 0 to 12
metre: 0 to 2 m
ft./yd.: 0 to 2 yd.

**Weight**

grams: 0 to 1 kg (100, 200, 300, 400, 500, 600, 700, 800, 900)
oz.: 0, 4, 8, 12, 1 lb., 20, 24, 28, 2 lb.

**COURTESIES.** See also BOY MEETS GIRL. Most of the precepts for getting along with people anywhere apply to Yugoslavia—be friendly, be yourself, be reasonable. If the locals put ice-cubes in their drinks and you don't, or vice versa, don't let it keep you awake at night.

Speaking of drinks, if a Yugoslav offers you one, it's just about obligatory to accept. If you're not in the mood for brandy, say yes to coffee. You aren't expected to stand the next round; the hospitality can be returned at a later date. If you're a house guest or otherwise treated to a great deal of food, drink and kindness, you may reciprocate by buying a small gift, preferably for any children in the family. Children are very important in the Yugoslavian scheme of things. (Notice the young couples proudly promenading with their offspring.)

Handshaking, seemingly at every opportunity, is a "must" when greeting almost anybody.

All this old-fashioned central European courtesy (though we're in the Balkans, traces of the centuries of Austrian influence remain) is suddenly forgotten in less-relaxed situations—such as clambering aboard an overcrowded bus. *Izvinite* (excuse me) is about all one can say.

Always ask permission before taking photos of people.

| | |
|---|---|
| Good day/Good afternoon. | **Dobar dan.** |

**CREDIT CARDS and TRAVELLERS' CHEQUES** *(kreditna karta; putni ček)*

**Credit cards:** Diner's Club and American Express are the most widely accepted cards. Although many hotels, restaurants and tourist-oriented enterprises accept credit cards, they're by no means known everywhere.

**Travellers' cheques:** These may be changed at banks, hotels and travel agencies and are accepted in many shops and restaurants. You'll almost certainly be asked to show your passport when cashing a cheque.

**Dinar cheques** are cheques made out in dinars that foreigners can use for most kinds of goods and services within the country (any difference between the value of the cheque and the service rendered is made up in change). Unused cheques must be changed back into convertible currency at the banks before leaving the country together with the original receipt issued by the bank or currency-exchange office.

| | |
|---|---|
| Do you accept travellers' cheques? | **Da li primate putne čekove?** |
| Can I pay with this credit card? | **Mogu li da platim kreditnom kartom?** |

**CRIME and THEFTS** *(zločin; kradja)*. If you need to report a theft or the like, and there's no policeman in sight, the nearest travel office or hotel desk should be able to put you in quick touch with the *milicija* (police).

Crime persists under all known social systems, so don't tempt fate by leaving your valuables imprudently unprotected or exposed.

| | |
|---|---|
| I want to report a theft. | **Želim da prijavim kradju.** |
| My... has been stolen. | **Meni su ukrali...** |
| handbag | **tašnu** |
| passport | **pasoš** |
| wallet | **novčanik [lisnicu]** |

**C** **CURRENCY** *(valuta)*. The monetary unit of Yugoslavia is the *dinar* (abbreviated *din*.).
Coins: 1, 2, 5, 10, 20, 50 and 100 dinars.
Banknotes: 10, 20, 50, 100, 500, 1,000, 2,000 and 5,000 dinars.

**CURRENCY EXCHANGE**—see **BANKS**

**CUSTOMS CONTROLS.** See also Entry Formalities. The best policy with customs men anywhere is to tell the truth if they ask any questions; being caught after replying "inexactly" could be embarrassing.

The following chart shows what main duty-free items you may take into Yugoslavia and, when returning home, into your own country:

| Into: | Cigarettes | | Cigars | | Tobacco | Spirits | | Wine |
|---|---|---|---|---|---|---|---|---|
| Yugoslavia | 200 | or | 50 | or | 250 g. | 1 l. | and | 1 l. |
| Canada | 200 | and | 50 | and | 900 g. | 1.1 l. | or | 1.1 l. |
| Eire | 200 | or | 50 | or | 250 g. | 1 l. | and | 2 l. |
| U.K. | 200 | or | 50 | or | 250 g. | 1 l. | and | 2 l. |
| U.S.A. | 200 | and | 100 | and | * | 1 l. | or | 1 l. |

\* A reasonable quantity.

While you may bring unlimited sums of foreign currency into Yugoslavia, you may not carry more than 5,000 dinars (in denominations no larger than 1,000 dinars) across the border in either direction, and this amount can only be imported or exported once per calendar year. On subsequent trips, a maximum of 2,000 dinars may be imported or exported.

Souvenirs and duty-free wine and tobacco products are sold at Yugoslavian airports.

| | |
|---|---|
| I've nothing to declare. | **Nemam ništa za carinjenje.** |
| It's for personal use. | **To je za moju ličnu upotrebu.** |

## DRIVING IN YUGOSLAVIA

**Entering Yugoslavia:** To take your car into Yugoslavia you'll need:

- A valid driving licence; an International Driving Licence is recommended but not required
- Car registration papers
- Green Card (international insurance certificate).

The nationality code sticker must be visible on the back of your car. You must have with you a red-reflector warning triangle in case of breakdown, a first-aid kit and a spare set of light bulbs. Seat belts are compulsory. Motorcycle or scooter drivers as well as passengers must wear helmets.

**Driving conditions:** Drive on the right and pass on the left; yield right of way to all vehicles coming from the right.

All resorts and most other places of interest are connected by asphalt roads. Secondary roads tend to be fairly narrow and winding; be certain you have a clear view ahead before attempting to overtake, or unforeseen obstructions such as pedestrians, donkeys or ox carts may catch you off guard. Quaint local attractions may become deadly perils on the road. When passing through villages, drive with extra care to avoid children darting out of doorways and older folk strolling in the middle of the road, particularly after dark. You'll need steely self-control to resist looking around at the spectacular scenery—it's better to stop more often and really enjoy the view.

There are very few toll roads in Yugoslavia, and none in the area around Split.

**Alcohol limit:** Yugoslavia has stringent regulations on drinking and driving, allowing only 50 milligrams per 100 millilitres of blood. Violations can lead to fines or even jail.

**Speed limits:** 60 kilometres per hour in town, 120 on motorways (expressways), 100 on main roads and 80 on other roads, unless otherwise indicated. If you're towing a caravan (trailer), you must not exceed 80 kilometres per hour.

**Traffic police** *(saobraćajna milicija)*: The traffic police wear grey-blue uniforms and, in summer, white helmets. Some cities employ white-uniformed students to help direct traffic and give information. Usually they speak at least one foreign language. Police cars, generally blue and white with a roof light, are often parked at busy road junctions. Dangerous driving may be treated very severely. For other infractions—such as ignoring a stop sign or breaking speed limits—the driver may be fined on the spot. The defendant is entitled to demand a court hearing, but this is a time-consuming way to prove a principle.

**Fuel and oil:** Not every crossroads boasts a filling station, but the coast is reasonably well supplied with them. Two grades of petrol (gasoline) are available: normal (86 octane) and super (98 octane). You'll also find diesel fuel.

**Petrol coupons:** These coupons can be bought at travel agencies, at automobile clubs in the country of departure, at the Yugoslav frontier or from an authorized exchange dealer in Yugoslavia, and mean a slight reduction in petrol prices. Unused coupons are refunded at the border when leaving the country or at the place where they were bought. N.B. Ask your automobile association about the latest regulations, as they are constantly changing.

Note that it is prohibited to enter Yugoslavia with a spare can of petrol in the car.

**Fluid measures**

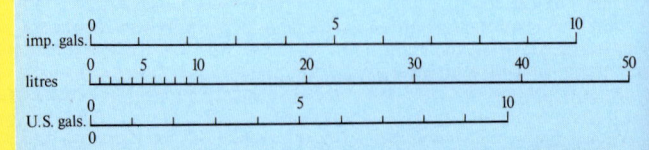

**Tire pressure**

| lb./sq. in. | kg/cm$^2$ | lb./sq. in. | kg/cm$^2$ |
|---|---|---|---|
| 10 | 0.7 | 26 | 1.8 |
| 12 | 0.8 | 27 | 1.9 |
| 15 | 1.1 | 28 | 2.0 |
| 18 | 1.3 | 30 | 2.1 |
| 20 | 1.4 | 33 | 2.3 |
| 21 | 1.5 | 36 | 2.5 |
| 23 | 1.6 | 38 | 2.7 |
| 24 | 1.7 | 40 | 2.8 |

**Distance**

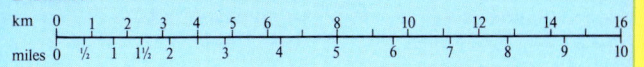

```
km    0    1    2    3    4    5    6       8      10     12      14      16
miles 0   ½    1   1½   2        3       4       5      6       7     8      9      10
```

**Breakdowns:** The Automobile Association of Yugoslavia (Auto-Moto Savez Jugoslavije, AMSJ) runs aid and information offices in major towns. They're open from 8 a.m. to 8 p.m. You can call on them for help in many towns, usually by dialling 987; rates charged for road and towing services are cheaper than those of garages.

Garages specializing in the repair of the leading makes of cars are found only in the larger cities. Privately run garages elsewhere can probably tide you over with ingenious stop-gap methods. But insist on a realistic price estimate in advance. If you need replacement parts there may be a problem of long delays. Spare parts are readily available for cars assembled in Yugoslavia: Citroën, Fiat, Renault, Volkswagen and the Zastava 101. The automobile association can help with urgent shipments and legal aid if you should need it. Naturally, an ounce of prevention—a thorough check of your car before you ever leave home—can avoid many a holiday headache on the road.

**Parking:** Fees vary. Some towns have a lot of free parking space, others charge a few dinars an hour in central locations. Incidentally, wherever you park—in towns or on a country road—the law requires that you park your car in the direction of moving traffic, on the right-hand side, never facing the flow of traffic. If you leave your car in a no-parking zone it may be towed away.

**Road signs:** The standard international picture signs are in general use throughout Yugoslavia. But here are a few of the more common written notices you may encounter:

| | |
|---|---|
| **Aerodrom** | Airport |
| **Automehaničar** | Car mechanic |
| **Centar grada** | Town centre |
| **Garaža** | Garage |
| **Milicija** | Police |
| **Opasna krivina** | Dangerous curve |
| **Opasnost** | Danger |
| **Radovi na putu** | Road works (Men working) |
| **Stoj** | Stop |
| **Škola** | School |
| **Uspon** | Steep hill |

**D**

| (International) Driving Licence | **(medjunarodna) vozačka dozvola** |
| Car registration papers | **saobraćajna dozvola** |
| Green Card | **zelena karta** |
| Are we on the right road for…? | **Da li je ovo put za…?** |
| Full tank please, top grade. | **Napunite molim Vas, super.** |
| Check the oil/tires/battery. | **Proverite ulje/gume/akumulator.** |
| I've had a breakdown. | **Kola su mi u kvaru.** |
| There's been an accident. | **Dogodio se nesrećni slučaj.** |

**DRUGS.** The authorities take a very dim view of anyone choosing Yugoslavia as a corridor for drug smuggling.

**E**

**ELECTRIC CURRENT** *(električna struja)*. The standard voltage in Yugoslavia is 220 volt, 50 cycle, A.C. American appliances will need transformers and plug adaptors.

If your hair-dryer or other electric appliance breaks down, ask your hotel desk-clerk if he can recommend an electrical repair shop or local handyman to rescue you.

I'd like an adaptor/a battery.   **Želim adaptor/bateriju.**

**EMERGENCIES.** Depending on the nature of the emergency, refer to the separate entries in this section such as CONSULATES, MEDICAL CARE, POLICE etc. If there's no time, put your problem into the hands of your hotel receptionist, travel agency or a taxi driver.

Though we hope you'll never need them, here are a few key words you might like to learn as insurance:

| Careful | **Oprezno** | Police | **Milicija** |
| Fire | **Vatra** | Stop | **Stanite** |
| Help | **U pomoć** | Stop thief | **Držite lopova** |

**ENTRY FORMALITIES.** See also CUSTOMS CONTROLS. All travellers must carry valid passports. Citizens of Great Britain and Ireland may enter Yugoslavia without visas or formalities. American and Canadian citizens are automatically given entry visas upon arrival. Of course, if in doubt about visa formalities, it's wise to check with your travel agent before you leave home.

Residents of the British Isles, continental Europe and North America need no health certificate to enter Yugoslavia. If you're coming from further afield you may need an international smallpox certificate, so check beforehand.

**EXCURSIONS** *(izlet)*. Every tourist office and hotel has day and half-day trips by bus or boat prominently advertised. Prices are invariably uniform: no need to shop around. If you feel like going alone, compare normal bus or steamer fares. It may be as convenient, and is certainly considerably cheaper, to use public transportation. This applies to shorter excursions and not to full-day organized trips visiting several places: a time-consuming and complicated chore to undertake unless you have your own car. Check if the tour price includes a meal, and, if not, order a picnic lunch the night before from your hotel receptionist.

It's wiser not to plan any sidetrips on the first and last days of July and August when everyone is going on holiday or returning, bumper to bumper.


**FIRE.** Forest fires are a real menace in summer so be very careful where you throw your cigarette butts and matches. Note that some zones—clearly marked—prohibit both smoking and open fires. If you're enjoying a legal campfire, don't forget to extinguish it and douse it with water before leaving.


**GUIDES and INTERPRETERS** *(vodič; tumač)*. The average tourist won't need any special assistance. Hotel personnel can deal with most linguistic problems, and the travel agencies provide competent multilingual guides to conduct their tours.

However, if you need personalized interpreting or guidance for business or pleasure, apply to one of the travel agencies in the nearest city or resort.

| | |
|---|---|
| We'd like an English-speaking guide. | **Hteli bismo engleskog vodiča.** |
| I need an English interpreter. | **Trebam tumača za engleski jezik.** |


**HAGGLING** *(cenkanje)*. Almost without exception, shops in Yugoslavia post their prices and stick by them; haggling might be considered offensive. But if you're shopping for souvenirs at outdoor bazaars or from pushcart-pedlars, by all means try to negotiate a better price.


**HAIRDRESSER'S** *(frizer)*. Prices are more than double if you patronize establishments in luxury hotels rather than neighbourhood shops.

**H** Tip about 10 per cent.

| | |
|---|---|
| haircut | **šišanje** |
| shave | **brijanje** |
| shampoo and set | **pranje kose i češljanje** |
| permanent wave | **trajna ondulacija** |
| colour chart | **pregled boja** |
| colour rinse | **preliv** |
| manicure | **manikir** |

| | |
|---|---|
| Don't cut it too short. | **Nemojte suviše visiko.** |
| A little more off (here). | **Odrežite još malo (ovde).** |
| How much do I owe you? | **Koliko sam dužan?** |

**HEALTH.** Many tourists who suffer health problems in Yugoslavia have only themselves to blame—for overdoing the sunshine and inexpensive alcohol. If you want to protect a delicate stomach, take it easy on the adventurous foods for the first few days and stick to the excellent mineral waters. See also EMERGENCIES and MEDICAL CARE.

**HITCH-HIKING** *(autostop)*. It's permitted but it isn't always carefree. A high percentage of passing cars are loaded with passengers and luggage.

| | |
|---|---|
| Can you give us a lift to...? | **Možete li nas povesti do...?** |

**HOTELS and ACCOMMODATION** *(hotel; smeštaj)*. Hotels in Yugoslavia are officially graded in five categories. L is de luxe and from there the classifications descend from A to D, the latter being the lowest grade which earns the title hotel. The classifications are designed to give you an idea of what facilities are offered and what they should cost.

Luxury hotels, extremely rare, measure up to the highest international standards. Full board in a luxury hotel may cost twice as much as the room rate in a slightly less elegant A-class hotel. Unless half or full board is part of the room rate, breakfast isn't generally included.

Rates go down about 40 per cent off season. Every traveller staying in a hotel or camping area pays a tourist tax; the amount depends upon season and local regulations.

**Other forms of accommodation:**

A **pansion** (boarding house) sometimes has fewer facilities than a hotel. They're graded in three categories: I to III. Prices run about the same as C category hotels.

A **turističko naselje** ("tourist village") may consist of bungalows or pavilions sprawling around a central core of restaurants and public rooms.

A **motel** is sometimes tied in with car repair facilities and is found along Yugoslav highways.

A **stan** or **vila** (apartment/villa) is a popular holiday accommodation for many visitors to Yugoslavia but may be difficult to arrange at the last moment. Write to the tourist office of the resort of your choice for information.

A **soba** (room) in a private home can usually be arranged at a local tourist office. These often outnumber hotel rooms, and are closely supervised and graded (from I to IV) according to comfort and location. Landladies canvassing near ferry and bus terminals often offer rooms which haven't been registered with the local authorities and which may or may not be up to standard.

Whether all your problems have been solved far in advance by a package-tour operator, or you arrive without any warning, housing can certainly be arranged. However, at the height of the season the unexpected visitor may have to settle for an extremely modest roof over his head.

| | |
|---|---|
| a double/single room | **soba sa dva kreveta/sa jednim krevetom** |
| with/without bath | **sa kupatilom/bez kupatila** |
| What's the rate per night? | **Koliko staje za jednu noć?** |

**HOURS** (see also BANKS and POST OFFICES)

**Consulates/Embassies** are usually open from 8 or 8.30 a.m. to 12.30 or 1 p.m. and reopen between 1.30—3.30 to 5 p.m., Monday to Friday (some close in the afternoon on certain weekdays).

**Offices:** 7 a.m. to 2 or 3 p.m., Monday to Friday.

**Shops:** 8 a.m. to noon and 5 to 8 p.m., Monday to Friday, 8 a.m. to 2 or 3 on Saturdays. Most self-service shops, department stores and food shops, however, are open non-stop.

**INTERPRETERS**—see **GUIDES**

**LANGUAGE.** Few countries can claim a more confusing linguistic situation. In Yugoslavia there are three major languages with equal status and two alphabets: the Latin one to which we're accustomed and the Cyrillic, similar to Russian.

All along the Dalmatian Coast as far south as the Bay of Kotor the language is Serbo-Croatian, which is spoken in most of the country. Yugoslavia's other two languages are Slovenian (spoken in the northwest) and Macedonian (spoken in the south-east). These three languages closely resemble one another. (Other languages—Albanian, Bulgarian, Hungarian, Romanian, Slovak and Turkish—are used by minorities in different regions of the nation.)

Nowadays English is the most widely understood foreign language along the coast, with German and Italian not too far behind. On a brief visit to Yugoslavia the most useful tool is Serbo-Croatian, understood by practically everyone in the country. A few words of that language will go a long way towards producing a smile and friendship.

| | |
|---|---|
| Good morning | **Dobro jutro** |
| Good day/Good afternoon | **Dobar dan** |
| Good evening | **Dobro veče** |
| Thank you | **Hvala** |
| You're welcome | **Nema na čemu** |
| Please | **Molim** |
| Goodbye | **Zbogom** |

The Berlitz phrase book SERBO-CROATIAN FOR TRAVELLERS covers almost all situations you're likely to encounter in your travels in Yugoslavia.

Does anybody here speak English?  **Da li neko ovde govori engleski?**

**LAUNDRY and DRY-CLEANING** *(pranje rublja; hemijsko čišćenje)*. Most hotels will handle your laundry and dry-cleaning relatively swiftly. Otherwise, you can go to a local laundry or dry-cleaner's, which in any case will be cheaper.

| | |
|---|---|
| I want these clothes... | **Želim ove stvari da se...** |
| cleaned/washed/ironed | **očiste/operu/ispeglaju** |
| When will it be ready? | **Kada će biti gotovo?** |
| I must have this for tomorrow morning. | **Ovo mi treba za sutra ujutro.** |

**LAWYERS and LEGAL SERVICES** *(advokat; pravna usluga)*. In case of serious trouble, ask your consulate or embassy for advice.

If your problem stems from a road mishap and you're a member of a motoring or touring association at home, free legal advice may be obtained from the Automobile Association of Yugoslavia.

**LOST AND FOUND PROPERTY** *(biro za nadjene stvari)*; **LOST CHILDREN.** Inquire first at your hotel reception desk or the nearest tourist office. Then report the loss to the *milicija* (police).

As for lost children, hotel personnel are accustomed to these crises and will help with sympathy and knowledgeable action.

| | |
|---|---|
| I've lost my wallet. | **Izgubio sam novčanik [lisnicu].** |
| I've lost my handbag. | **Izgubila sam tašnu.** |

**MAIL** *(pošta)*. If you're uncertain of your holiday address, you may have letters sent to you care of poste restante (general delivery) at some convenient post office. Mail should be addressed as follows:

> Mr. John Smith
> Post Restant
> Split
> Yugoslavia

The Split post office is at I. L. Lavčevića 9, and poste restante may be collected at window 10 between 7 a.m. and 9 p.m. When claiming your mail, you must produce your passport as identification. There is a small charge. See also POST OFFICE.

Have you any mail for me?   **Ima li pošte za mene?**

**MAPS** *(plan; karta)*. Yugoslav National Tourist Offices in your country issue free maps pinpointing resort areas.

On the spot, bookshops along the coast sell maps with greater detail. For the most serious explorers, the Yugoslav Lexicographical Institute has produced *The Yugoslav Coast, Guide Book and Atlas*. This impressively researched book contains listings for hundreds of towns and villages, plus 27 maps.

| | |
|---|---|
| a street plan of… | **plan grada…** |
| a road map of this region | **cestovna karta ovog kraja** |

**M** **MEDICAL CARE** *(lekarska usluga)*. See also EMERGENCIES. Citizens of half a dozen western European countries—including Great Britain—are entitled to free medical care under reciprocal agreements with Yugoslavia. Citizens of other countries must pay for medical services.

For help in minor emergencies, look for an *ambulanta* (first-aid post) displaying a red cross or an *apoteka* or *ljekarna* (chemist's, or drugstore). In Split, the latter take turns doing all-night duty *(dežurna ljekarna)*.

**Pharmacies.** In an *apoteka* you'll find both non-prescription medicines and those made up according to a prescription. In a *drogerija* you'll find a great range of toilet articles, cosmetics and the like, sometimes films, too.

In the window of an *apoteka* you'll see a notice telling you where the nearest all-night chemist is. In larger towns, some chemists are open day and night. Their names and addresses can be found in daily newspapers.

If you're required to take certain medicine regularly, it would be wise to stock up before you leave home. Specific brands of medicine might not always be available locally in Yugoslavia.

| | |
|---|---|
| a doctor | **lekar [doktor]** |
| a dentist | **zubar [dentist]** |
| an ambulance | **kola za hitnu pomoć** |
| hospital | **bolnica** |
| an upset stomach | **pokvaren stomak** |
| sunstroke | **sunčanica** |
| a fever | **groznica** |

**N** **NEWSPAPERS and MAGAZINES** *(novine; časopis)*. Most leading western European newspapers, including British dailies and the American *International Herald Tribune* published in Paris, are sold at all major resorts. The papers usually arrive the day after publication. Popular foreign magazines are also sold at the same shops or stands.

Bookshops in the larger towns sell paperbacks in English and some other foreign languages but the selection is limited.

| | |
|---|---|
| Have you any English-language newspapers? | **Imate li novine na engleskom?** |

**P** **PETS and VETS.** Though *you* may not need a health certificate to enter Yugoslavia, your dog or cat won't be allowed across the border without one. This must attest to the animal's good health, include a vaccination record and affirm that you'll submit the pet to an examination by a Yugoslav vet at the border.

In many resort areas, if you need a vet you may find he's more attuned to the needs of mules and goats than chihuahuas.

Returning to Great Britain or Eire, your pet will have to undergo six months of quarantine. Both the U.S.A. and Canada reserve the right to impose quarantine.

**PHOTOGRAPHY** *(fotografisanje)*. You can buy film everywhere in Yugoslavia but to be sure of having your favourite brand, and to save on cost, bring your own supply from home. Photo shops in cities and even small towns advertise speedy developing. For colour film, though, it's probably faster to take your exposed film back home with you for development.

Certain areas—generally near military installations and national borders—are off limits to photographers. They're clearly marked with signs depicting an old-fashioned bellows camera crossed out with a diagonal red line.

Beware of lighting situations you might not have encountered before—especially the blinding reflections from the sea and white buildings. You may not be able to rely on the electric eye on your automatic camera in these situations. The secret is to compensate for the reflections with a faster shutter speed. Read your instruction book carefully or, before leaving home, talk over the problem with your camera dealer.

To protect your films against possible damage from x-rays at airport security checkpoints, put them in lead-coated plastic bags, available at photo shops in your own country.

| | |
|---|---|
| I'd like a film for this camera. | **Želim film za ovu kameru.** |
| a black-and-white film | **crno-beli film** |
| a colour film | **u boji [kolor] film** |
| a colour-slide film | **film za kolor dijapozitive** |
| 35-mm film | **trideset pet milimetarski film** |
| super-8 | **super osam** |
| How long will it take to develop (and print) this? | **Koliko vremena treba da se razvije film (i izrade fotografije)?** |

**POLICE** *(milicija)*. The national police, armed and wearing grey-blue uniforms, maintain public order and control traffic. Each policeman's

**P** identity is revealed by his service number, clearly engraved on his belt buckle. In Split the telephone number is 92.

| Where's the nearest police station? | **Gde je najbliža milicijska stanica?** |
|---|---|

**POST OFFICE and TELEGRAMS** (*pošta; telegram*). Most post offices are open from 7 a.m. to 8 p.m. without a break, though some operate on a reduced schedule, say from 8 a.m. to 1 p.m. and from 5 to 8 p.m. Post offices also handle long-distance telephone calls (see TELEPHONE) and telegrams, which can also be sent by phone from your hotel. The main post office in Split, at Lavčevića 9, has a 24-hour telegram service.

You can buy stamps at tobacconists' and some news-stands as well.

Airmail is recommended to all destinations unless time isn't essential. Registered letters and packages must be presented unsealed; the postal clerk will seal them in your presence.

Letterboxes in Yugoslavia, painted yellow, are usually affixed to house walls. Post offices have yellow PTT signs outside.

| express (special delivery) | **ekspres** |
|---|---|
| airmail | **avionom** |
| registered | **preporučeno** |
| poste restante (general delivery) | **post restant** |
| A stamp for this letter/postcard, please. | **Molim Vas marku za ovo pismo/ za ovu kartu.** |
| I want to send a telegram to... | **Želim da pošaljem telegram za...** |

**PRICES.** The following are some prices in Yugoslav dinars/U.S. dollars. However, they must be regarded as approximate and taken as broad guidelines; inflation in Yugoslavia, as elsewhere, rises steadily.

**Airport departure tax.** Domestic flights 300 din., international 1,000 din.

**Camping.** U.S.$3.50 per person per night, $1.30 for tent or car, $2 per caravan (trailer).

**Car hire.** *Renault 4* U.S.$16.50 per day, 17¢ per km., $220 per week with unlimited mileage. *Zastava 128* $22 per day, 22¢ per km., $305 per week with unlimited mileage. *Opel Kadett* $37 per day, 37¢ per km., $483 per week with unlimited mileage. Add 15% tax and insurance.

**Entertainment.** Discotheque 160–600 din., cinema 100–160 din. depending on length of film, orchestral concerts 300–2,000 din., folklore performances 2,000 din. (transport included).

**Hairdressers.** *Woman's* shampoo and set 900 din., shampoo and blow-dry 1,000 din., permanent wave 1,500 din. *Man's* haircut 400 din.

**Meals and drinks.** Continental breakfast 470 din., lunch/dinner (in a fairly good establishment) 1,400 din., coffee 140 din., Yugoslav brandy and most Yugoslav spirits 140 din., litre of local wine 660 din., soft drinks 170 din.

| | |
|---|---|
| Is there an admission charge? | **Koliko staje ulaz?** |
| How much? | **Koliko staje?** |
| Have you something cheaper? | **Imate li nešto jeftinije?** |

## PUBLIC HOLIDAYS *(državni praznik)*

| | | |
|---|---|---|
| Jan. 1, 2 | *Nova godina* | New Year |
| May 1, 2 | *Prvi maj* | Labour Days |
| July 4 | *Dan borca* | Veterans' Day |
| Nov. 29, 30 | *Dan Republike* | Republic Days |

In addition, a Day of the Uprising *(Dan Ustanka)* is celebrated in Croatia on July 27.

| | |
|---|---|
| Are you open tomorrow? | **Da li je otvoreno sutra?** |

**RADIO and TV** *(radio; televizija)*. Two Yugoslav television channels serve the area. Feature films are usually shown with the original sound-track and subtitles. You don't have to understand Serbo-Croatian to follow sports or musical shows.

On medium-wave radio, the local programmes of a good many European countries are easily picked up on any transistor. BBC and Voice of America programmes are heard most clearly on short wave in the early morning and at night.

In summer, Zagreb radio has a daily English-language broadcast for tourists with news and helpful information.

**S** **SEAMSTRESSES and TAILORS** *(krojačica; krojač)*. If your clothing suddenly needs minor alterations, ask your hotel maid or desk-clerk to send it out for repairs. If you're more adventurous—or desperate—take the problem to the nearest town. There's no shortage of tailors; you can see them sewing in their ground-floor workrooms facing the street.

| Could you mend this by tomorrow evening? | **Možete li popraviti ovo do sutra uveče?** |
|---|---|

**T** **TAXIS** *(taksi)*. Clearly marked taxis are available at ranks in all towns and tourist centres. In larger towns taxis have meters, but in smaller places, where there may be only one taxi, it's a good idea to ask about the fare in advance. Extra charges are levied for luggage and night travel.

The telephone number for taxis in Split is: 47-777.

| What's the fare to…? | **Koliko košta do…?** |
|---|---|


**TELEGRAMS**—see **POST OFFICES**


**TELEPHONE** *(telefon)*. Most towns have telephones on the street from which you may dial local calls by depositing 2 dinars.

For long-distance calls, the telephone office is located in the local post office. In most localities in Yugoslavia, you can dial direct to western Europe. Or, if you prefer, your hotel switchboard should be able to handle any calls, local or international.

If you're having difficulty spelling names, use this foolproof Yugoslavian telephone alphabet:

| A | Avala | F | Foča | N | Niš | V | Valjevo |
|---|---|---|---|---|---|---|---|
| B | Beograd | G | Gorica | Nj | Njegoš | Z | Zagreb |
| C | Cetinje | H | Hercegovina | O | Osijek | Ž | Žirovnica |
| Č | Čačak | I | Istra | P | Pirot | | |
| Ć | Ćuprija | J | Jadran | R | Rijeka | Q | Kvadrat |
| D | Dubrovnik | K | Kosovo | S | Skopje | W | Duplo V |
| Dž | Džamija | L | Lika | Š | Šibenik | X | Iks |
| Dj | Djakovo | Lj | Ljubljana | T | Titograd | Y | Ipsilon |
| E | Evropa | M | Mostar | U | Uroševac | | |

Some useful numbers:

| | |
|---|---|
| Police | 92 |
| Fire | 93 |
| Ambulance | 94 |
| Telegrams | 96 |
| Inquiries | 988 |
| General information | 981 |

The international access code from Yugoslavia is 99. Some country codes: Canada/USA 1, Ireland 353, UK 44. Area codes for principal Yugoslav towns: Belgrade 011, Ljubljana 061, Niš 018, Rijeka 051, Skopje 091, Split 058, Zagreb 041.

| | |
|---|---|
| May I use your telephone? | **Mogu li se poslužiti Vašim telefonom?** |
| Can you help me get this number? | **Hoćete li mi nazvati ovaj broj?** |

**TIME DIFFERENCES.** Yugoslavia sticks to Central European Time (GMT +1) as does most of the Continent. In summer, the clock is put one hour ahead (GMT +2):

| Los Angeles | Chicago | New York | London | **Split** |
|---|---|---|---|---|
| 4 a.m. | 6 a.m. | 7 a.m. | noon | **1 p.m.** |

**TIPPING.** Hotel bills are all-inclusive. Though restaurant bills feature a 10 per cent service charge, it is usual to tip the waiter 5 to 10 per cent.

Further recommendations:

| | |
|---|---|
| Barber/Hairdresser | 10% |
| Lavatory attendant | 5–10 din. |
| Maid, per week | 300 din. |
| Porter, per bag | 50 din. |
| Taxi driver | optional |
| Tourist guide | 5–10% |

**TOILETS.** Though public conveniences aren't very widely distributed or advertised, you need look no farther than the nearest hotel, restaurant or bar.

The facilities are usually marked by symbols rather than words *(muški* for men and *ženski* for women).

The symbols are either a silhouette of a flat shoe for men and a high-heeled shoe for women or the more conventional stick figures of a man or a woman.

| Where are the toilets? | **Gde je VC** (pronounced *ve-tse*) **molim Vas?** |
|---|---|

**TOURIST-INFORMATION OFFICES** *(turistički biro)*. In major cities of Europe and America, Yugoslav National Tourist Offices offer complete information to help you plan your holiday. They'll also let you consult a copy of the master directory of hotels in Yugoslavia, listing all facilities and rates. Among the addresses:

**British Isles:** 143, Regent St., London W.1.; tel.: (01) 734-5243

**U.S.A.:** 630 Fifth Ave., New York, NY 10022; tel.: (212) 757-2801.

The offices can supply maps, leaflets and brochures on general or specialized subjects about Yugoslavia.

Once on the spot you'll find municipal tourist-information offices in all the major resorts. The Tourist-Information Office in Split is at Titova obala 12; tel.: 42-142.

Travel-agency offices also stand ready to answer your questions. Some of the agencies you'll encounter in Adriatic resorts are Atlas, Centroturist, Dalmacijaturist, Generalturist, Kompas, Putnik and Yugotours.

**TRAINS** *(vlak [voz])*. If you're keen on spectacular scenery and have about nine hours to spare, you can reach Split from Zagreb or Belgrade by rail. Locally, buses and boats provide more comprehensive transportation (see BUS SERVICES and BOAT SERVICES).

The priority and speed of a train is indicated by its category—local *(putnički)*, inter-city *(poslovni)*, fast *(brzi)* and express *(ekspresni)*. In season, trains tend to be crowded; it's wise to book seats and sleeping accommodation in advance.

The railway station *(kolodvor)* in Split is located on Obala Bratstva Jedinstva near the bus terminal and steamer moorings, so connections for further points are easy.

**TRAVELLERS' CHEQUES**—see **CREDIT CARDS**

**WATER** *(voda)*. You may quaff with confidence from the carafe on your café table. But while the drink is safe, the change in mineral content in any unaccustomed water may disturb delicate stomachs. If you're sensitive, stick to bottled mineral water *(mineralna voda* or *kisela voda)*. It's cheap and tasty.

| | |
|---|---|
| a bottle of mineral water | **flašu mineralne vode** |
|   carbonated | **gazirane** |
|   non-carbonated | **ne gazirane** |
| Is this drinking water? | **Da li je ovo voda za piće?** |

**YOUTH and STUDENT HOSTELS** *(omladinsko/studentsko letovalište)*. You can obtain a list of Yugoslav hostels and their facilities from your own national youth-hostels association. A few hostels stay open all year round, but most of them operate in the summer months only. In central Dalmatia, they're located along the coast at Zadar, Šibenik, Kaštel Gomilica, Rogač-Omiš, Baška Voda and Makarska. Sleeping bags aren't available for hire, nor are cooking facilities provided. There's no age limit, but priority is given to visitors under 27.

Group bookings, as well as organized holidays and travel for young people, are coordinated by the Bureau for the International Exchange of Youth and Students, Moše Pijade 12, Belgrade. Individual bookings should be made directly with the pertinent hostel or the association running it.

## DAYS OF THE WEEK

| Sunday | **nedelja** | Thursday | **četvrtak** |
| Monday | **ponedeljak** | Friday | **petak** |
| Tuesday | **utorak** | Saturday | **subota** |
| Wednesday | **sreda** | | |

## MONTHS

| January | **januar** | July | **jul** |
| February | **februar** | August | **avgust** |
| March | **mart** | September | **septembar** |
| April | **april** | October | **oktobar** |
| May | **maj** | November | **novembar** |
| June | **jun** | December | **decembar** |

## NUMBERS

| 0 | **nula** | 18 | **osamnaest** |
| 1 | **jedan** | 19 | **devetnaest** |
| 2 | **dva** | 20 | **dvadeset** |
| 3 | **tri** | 21 | **dvadeset jedan** |
| 4 | **četiri** | 22 | **dvadeset dva** |
| 5 | **pet** | 30 | **trideset** |
| 6 | **šest** | 31 | **trideset jedan** |
| 7 | **sedam** | 40 | **četrdeset** |
| 8 | **osam** | 50 | **pedeset** |
| 9 | **devet** | 60 | **šezdeset** |
| 10 | **deset** | 70 | **sedamdeset** |
| 11 | **jedanaest** | 80 | **osamdeset** |
| 12 | **dvanaest** | 90 | **devedeset** |
| 13 | **trinaest** | 100 | **sto** |
| 14 | **četrnaest** | 101 | **sto jedan** |
| 15 | **petnaest** | 102 | **sto dva** |
| 16 | **šesnaest** | 500 | **pet stotina** |
| 17 | **sedamnaest** | 1,000 | **jedna hiljada** |

## SOME USEFUL EXPRESSIONS

| | |
|---|---|
| yes/no | da/ne |
| please/thank you | molim/hvala |
| excuse me/you're welcome | izvinite/molim |
| | |
| where/when/how | gde/kad/kako |
| how long/how far | koliko dugo/koliko daleko |
| yesterday/today/tomorrow | jučer/danas/sutra |
| day/week/month/year | dan/nedelja/mesec/godina |
| | |
| left/right | levo/desno |
| up/down | gore/dole |
| good/bad | dobro/loše |
| big/small | veliko/malo |
| cheap/expensive | jeftino/skupo |
| hot/cold | vruće/hladno |
| old/new | staro/novo |
| open/closed | otvoreno/zatvoreno |

Is there anyone here who speaks English? — **Da li ima neko ko govori engleski?**

I don't understand. — **Ne razumem.**

Please speak more slowly. — **Molim Vas govorite polaganije.**

Please write is down. — **Molim Vas napišite mi to.**

What does this mean? — **Šta ovo znači?**

What do you want? — **Šta želite?**

Just a minute. — **Samo trenutak.**

What time is it? — **Koliko je sati?**

Which is the road to...? — **Koji je put za...?**

Waiter, please. — **Konobar, molim.**

I'd like... — **Želeo bih...**

How much is that? — **Koliko staje?**

Help me please. — **Pomozite mi, molim Vas.**

Get a doctor—quickly! — **Zovite doktora–brzo!**

Where are the toilets? — **Gde su toaleti?**

# Index

An asterisk (*) next to a page number indicates a map reference.

Adriatic Highway  8, 26*, 30, 31*, 55, 56*, 58
Alexander, King of Yugoslavia  15
Aqueducts  27, 43
Austrians  12–14, 19, 32, 36, 37

Bačvice  26*, 26
Baščaršija  62
Baška Voda  56*, 58
Beaches  7, 26, 44, 50, 53, 64, 67
Benkovac  31*, 45, 74
Betina  42
Biograd Na Moru  12, 31*, 44–45
Biokovo Mountains  7, 56*, 58
Biševo  56*, 69
Blue Grotto  69
Bol  56*, 64
Borik  50
Brač Island  7–8, 56*, 57, 63–64
Brela  7, 56*, 58

Camping  42, 52, 101
Cetina River  31*, 55
Chapel of St. John Orsini (Trogir)  34
Children's activities  77–78
Churches
 Sveta Stošija (Zadar)  45*, 47–48
 Sveti Donat (Zadar)  45*, 46
 Sveti Dujam (Split)  19*, 21–22
 Sveti Jakov (Šibenik)  37*, 37
 Sveti Krševan (Zadar)  45*, 48
 Sveti Lovrijenac (Trogir)  32–34
 Sveti Marko (Korčula)  70
 Sveti Stjepan (Hvar)  67
 Svi Sveti – see Guildhall
Čiovo  31*, 34, 56*
Čipiko Palace (Trogir)  34
Climate  8–9, 64–65, 97
Corfu Declaration  14, 15
Croatia  11–13, 14, 28, 45, 46, 50–51
Crvena Luka  44

Dalmatia  6, 11–13, 45, 47
Dalmatinac, Juraj  22, 24, 38, 41, 53
Dernek  30
Diocletian, Emperor  6, 18, 26
Diocletian's Palace (Split)  6, 18–21, 19*, 26*, 64, 74
Dragon's Cave – see Murvica
Dubrovnik  8, 56*, 74
Dugi otok  31*, 54

Fauna  72, 84
Ferry boats  8, 42, 63, 96, 100
Festivals  30, 74–75
Films  76
Fishing  43, 52, 72, 82
Flora  84
Folklore  28, 30, 72, 73–74
Food  85–94
Fort of St. Anne (Šibenik)  41
Fort Wellington  56*, 70

Fortress of Kamerlengo (Trogir) 35
Foša 45*, 49
Franz Ferdinand, Archduke 14, 62

Gata 55, 56*
Gradac 56*, 60
Greeks 11, 32, 68
Guard House – see Museums, Ethnographic (Zadar)
Guildhall (Korčula) 71

Hapsburgs – see Austrians
Hektorović, Petar 68
Hitler, Adolf 15
Hotels 8, 42, 50, 52, 67 112–114, 124
Hvar Island 9, 11, 56*, 58, 64–68
Hvar (town) 56*, 66–68

Illyrians 11, 13, 65
Imotski 56*, 57
Iž Islands 31*, 54

Jadranska Magistrale – see Adriatic Highway
Jadro River 26*, 27, 31*
Jelsa 56*, 68

Kačić-Miošić, Andrija 58
Kardeljevo 60
Karin Sea 51
Klis 28, 31*, 56*
Korana River 52
Korčula Island 8, 56*, 69–72, 73, 74
Korčula (town) 56*, 70–72
Kornati Islands 31*, 42
Kozjak, Lake 52
Kozjak Mountains 18, 28, 31*
Krapanj 36

Krka Falls 31*, 41
Krka River 31*, 36, 37*, 41
Kružić, Petar 28

Lun 53

Makarska 7, 56*, 58
Makarska Riviera 57, 60
Marco Polo 72
Marjan 26*, 26, 27
Markets 48, 49, 63
Marulić, Marko 24
Meštrović, Ivan 22, 24–26, 34, 38, 51, 55
Mihajlović, Draža 16
Miljacka River 62
Milna 64
More, Thomas 57
Mosor Mountains 18, 28, 56*
Mosques 28, 60
  Gazi Husref Beg (Sarajevo) 62
  Karadjoz Beg (Mostar) 60
Mostar 56*, 60–61
Murter 31*, 42
Murvica 56*, 64
Museums 76–77
  Abbot's Palace (Korčula) 71
  Archaeological (Split) 26*, 27
  Archaeological (Zadar) 46
  Ethnographic (Split) 24
  Ethnographic (Zadar) 45*, 46
  Maritime (Split) 26
  Meštrović Gallery (Split) 25, 26, 26*
  Palača Papalić (Split) 19*, 24
  Regional Museum (Sarajevo) 62–63
  Town Museum (Šibenik) 37*, 41

**INDEX**

**127**

# INDEX

Napoleon   *12–13, 65*
Neretva River   *56\*, 60*
Nicholas of Florence   *34, 38*
Nightlife   *67, 75*
Nin   *31\*, 50, 51*
Novalja   *53*
Novigrad   *31\*, 51*
Novigrad Sea   *51, 52*

Obrovac   *31\*, 51*
Omiš   *55, 56\*, 74*

Pag Island   *31\*, 52–53*
Pag (town)   *52–53*
Pakleni Islets   *56\*, 67*
Pakoštane   *44*
Palmižana   *67*
Partisans   *16, 19, 46*
Paul, Prince of Yugoslavia   *15*
Peristyle   *19\*, 21*
Peter, King of Yugoslavia   *16*
Plitvice National Park   *31\*, 51–52*
Počitelj   *56\*, 60*
Podgora   *7, 56\*, 58*
Posedarije   *31\*, 52*
Povja   *64*
Primošten   *31\*, 35*
Princip, Gavrilo   *62*
Promajna   *58*
Prvić   *31\*, 42*
Pučišća   *56\*, 64*

Ribar, Ivo Lola   *46*
Romans   *11, 27, 46, 65*
Rosandić, Toma   *64*

Salona   *11, 18, 27, 32*
Sarajevo   *14, 56\*, 60, 62*
Sedam Kaštela   *26\*, 30*
Serbia   *13, 14, 15*

Shakespeare, William   *27*
Shopping   *68, 78–80*
Šibenik   *24, 31\*, 36–41, 37\*, 74*
Sinj   *28, 31\*, 56\*, 74*
Slovenia   *11, 14*
Solin   *26\*, 27*
Španjolo Fortress (Hvar)   *67*
Spliska   *64*
Split   *7, 18–27, 19\*, 31\*, 56\*, 74*
Sports   *43, 72, 81–83*
Stari Grad   *56\*, 68*
Supetar   *56\*, 63*
Sutivan   *56\*, 63*

Tito, Josip Broz   *16, 19, 69*
Tomislav, King of Croatia   *12*
Trogir   *7, 12, 30–35, 31\*, 56\*, 74*
Turks   *12, 18, 28, 37, 45, 60, 67*

Ugljan   *31\*, 54*
Uskoks   *28*

Venice   *12, 32*
Vidova Gora   *64*
Vis Island   *11, 56\*, 68–69*
Visovac   *31\*, 41*
Vodice   *31\*, 42, 74*
Vrana Lake   *43, 82*
Vrančić, Faust   *42*
Vrboska   *56\*, 68*
Vrlika   *30, 31\*, 75*

Wine   *36, 57, 68, 85, 87, 90–91*

Zadar   *7, 8, 12, 31\*, 45\*, 45–50, 74, 75*
Zadvarje   *56\*, 57*
Zlarin   *31\*, 42*
Zrmanja River   *31\*, 51*

068/608 SUD